D1139330

MAKING A GARDEN

City and Guilds Leisurecraft Books

SERIES EDITOR: ALAN TITCHMARSH

MAKING A GARDEN

David Stevens

WORLD'S WORK LTD

All photographs are by the author

Design by Victor Shreeve

Illustration by
Pauline and David Stevens
Peter Snowball, John Spencer, Victor Shreeve

Published in conjunction with
City and Guilds of London Institute
by World's Work Ltd
The Windmill Press
Kingswood, Tadworth, Surrey

Copyright © 1984 David Stevens

ISBN 0 437 02401 6
Printed in Great Britain by BAS Printers Limited
Over Wallop, Stockbridge, Hampshire

CONTENTS

TABLES OF IMPERIAL/METRIC MEASUREMENT EQUIVALENTS

LENGTH		WEIGHT		VOLUME	
Imperial	*Metric*	*Imperial*	*Metric*	*Imperial*	*Metric*
$\frac{1}{8}$ in	0.3 cm	$\frac{1}{2}$ oz	14.2 g	$\frac{1}{2}$ pt	0.3 litre
$\frac{1}{4}$	0.6	1	28.4	1	0.6
$\frac{3}{8}$	1.0	$1\frac{1}{2}$	42.5	$1\frac{1}{2}$	0.9
$\frac{1}{2}$	1.3	2	56.7	2	1.2
$\frac{5}{8}$	1.6	$2\frac{1}{2}$	70.9	$2\frac{1}{2}$	1.5
$\frac{3}{4}$	1.9	3	85.1	3	1.8
$\frac{7}{8}$	2.2	$3\frac{1}{2}$	99.3	$3\frac{1}{2}$	2.1
1	2.5	4	113.4	4	2.4
2	5.0	6	170.1	5	3.0
3	7.5	8	226.8	6	3.6
4	10.0	10	283.5	7	4.2
5	12.5	12	340.8	8	4.8
6	15.0	14	397.6	9	5.4
7	17.5	1 lb	0.45 kg	10	6.0
8	20.0	2	0.91		
9	22.5	3	1.36		
10	25.0	4	1.81		
11	27.5	5	2.27		
1 ft	30.0	6	2.72		
$1\frac{1}{2}$	45.0	7	3.18		
2	60.0	8	3.63		
$2\frac{1}{2}$	75.0	9	4.08		
3	90.0	10	4.54		
4	1.2 m				
5	1.5				
10	3.0				
15	4.5				
20	6.0				
25	7.5				
30	9.0				

Preface

The making of a garden is a broad subject, comprising horticulture, design, constructional techniques and much more. The problem with most gardening books is that they dwell on one or two aspects without considering the picture as a whole, the creation of an outdoor room.

Making a garden must be a carefully thought-out process, starting with a survey of what you have and what you want, continuing through the design process, the evaluation of hard and soft surfaces and concluding with the furnishings that bring any composition to life. In between these broad categories lies a wealth of detail that needs careful handling, information that must be accurately correlated and cross-referred, as well as decisions that have to be made about the often confusing subject of plants.

The trouble is, of course, that we are continually bombarded with new catalogues of plants, shrubs and trees, while garden centres and nurseries are crammed full of every conceivable garden feature and furnishing. Overcomplication is the antithesis of good design and I have set out in this book the way the problem should be tackled, bearing in mind that it is you, the reader, who will stamp your personality on any design. Don't copy a garden design from this or any other book. Select ideas by all means, develop them certainly and by so doing create something that is unique and just right for you. And remember that the making of a garden need not be carried out all at one time: if you have a well thought-out plan you can implement the ideas over a period of several years even.

Throughout the book, in the sections dealing with design and construction and later on with the way plant material is handled, you will see that there are quite definite rules, many of which crop up time and time again. There is a great myth about gardening, and landscape designers in particular, that suggests that good gardens are brought about simply by spontaneous ideas, or even that nebulous attribute, 'greenfingers'. Nothing could be further from the truth. It cannot be emphasised enough that a good garden layout relies very heavily on a well thought-out planning sequence. It is just this that I analyse and invite you to try out for yourself.

This book does not deal with an individual subject, or even with 'gardening' in the conventional sense. It is, instead, an introduction and detailed guide to planning a room outside the house, in which the widest possible range of activities can take place. In the final analysis this room should serve you, and not the other way about. Of course, it will probably require some maintenance, but it can also be a place in which you can relax, play, grow fruit, flowers and vegetables as well as escape from the increasing pressures of everyday life.

Once you understand the basic rules, you can embark on a fascinating project – the creation of a new environment.

David Stevens

CHAPTER ONE

Basic assessments

Why do you need to design a garden?/What is a garden for?
What do you want in your garden?
What have you got in your garden already?
Checkpoint

WHY DO YOU NEED TO DESIGN A GARDEN?

Is it because

a you've just moved into a new house and want to create a garden;

b you've just moved into an old house and want to change the garden;

c you want to make your garden easier to manage;

d you want something more attractive to look at than a collection of dustbins, bikes, old sheds and washing lines, even though these must be included;

e you want to alter your existing garden because your family's needs have changed?

Whatever your reason, it will be unique to you and your garden, and the plans you make for changing your garden will also be unique. The whole process of designing a garden is an intensely personal affair. The prime reason why every garden is different is not because of inequalities of size, slope, aspect and locality but simply because no two people or families make the same demands on their garden. A site might be physically identical to its neighbour but because it serves different people it must offer different facilities. Therefore before you do anything at all to the layout of your garden, clarify your needs and note down your ideas.

WHAT IS A GARDEN FOR?

A garden is primarily for enjoyment. Think of it as an outdoor room serving the whole family in the widest possible way. This image will help you to shape and furnish your garden as you would a room in your house. If you find that you are quite competent and decisive at interior design – for a kitchen or lounge perhaps – but your ideas dry up when you move outside, the 'outdoor room' idea may help you too.

Many people are not 'gardeners' in the true sense of the word, nor do they want to be, but they still need to use the garden to its best advantage. The secret is to avoid being influenced by the traditional image of terraces, lawns, vegetables, fruit and other self-contained features that seem to be simply juggled about in a different order in every garden.

In part this is an historical problem. We have a preconceived idea of what a garden should be, which in many cases is an unconscious scaling-down of the much grander affairs our grandfathers knew. Gardens today, however, are not only smaller but have far greater demands put on them. No longer are they simply places in which to stroll and meditate; they now have to cater to the whims of adults, children, pets, friends and wildlife. Nor should the garden be out of bounds during the long winter: during favourable spells the well-designed garden should still offer scope for enjoyment.

Whether your garden is large or small, a barren builder's plot or an established composition that needs modification, the first job, before you even think of design, is to gather information. This falls into the two broad categories of what you want in the garden and what you have got there already.

WHAT DO YOU WANT IN YOUR GARDEN?

Make a list of the things that you and your family want in your garden. Do not hurry your decision-making. A garden that is built in a hurry is inevitably unsatisfactory and extra features are often tacked on at a later date. Not only does this create unnecessary expense but the extra features usually look like afterthoughts. Allow several months – the winter is ideal – and during this time jot down everything you can think of. It does not matter at this stage if the list seems endless because it can be rationalised later. The important thing is to leave nothing out.

If you have moved recently, another sound reason for not starting work too soon is simply to get used to your surroundings. It really takes a full year just to see what plants appear through the seasons and also to check on which parts of the garden receive sun or shade, shelter or wind. In today's age of technology this sort of information-gathering makes a worthwhile home computer program, in which the input can be updated and shuffled about at will!

A list for an average family (if there is such a thing) might include the following:

a A paved area for sitting and dining (see Chapter 5, 'Hard landscape') which would also provide room for housework (when mundane chores like ironing and preparing vegetables take on a new dimension!).

b Ample play space, taking the form of both lawn (see Chapter 6, 'Soft landscape') and harder surfaces for wheeled toys, sandpit, swings and washing line.

c Vegetables, shed and greenhouse, compost, bonfire and dustbins. (Remember that a garden has to encompass the ugly as well as the beautiful, and so any outdoor room worth its salt has to be highly practical.)

d Flowers for cutting, foliage for background (see Chapter 7, 'Plants and planting design'), formal and informal pools (see Chapter 8, 'Features and furnishings'), fruit, pets, badminton and cricket areas.

And so the list goes on. It can be very useful to draw up an actual checklist that includes the above and any other requirements you may have. A typical chart is set out in Table 1.1. By doing this you can see quickly the sort of emphasis and demands that are going to be relevant when you prepare a design (see Chapter 2, 'Designing your garden').

Table 1.1 **Garden checklist**

What do you have?	Answer
Any good or bad views	
Boundaries — type of fence or hedge	
Surfaces — gravel, concrete, brick etc	
Soil — acid/alkaline, heavy/light	
Interior floor/wall colours/materials in rooms adjoining garden	
Any changes in level	
Existing trees/planting	
Any other details	

What do you want? (tick as appropriate)			
Annuals		Swings/slide	
Roses		Dining area	
Herbaceous		Barbecue	
Shrubs		Pergola	
Ground cover		Paddling pool	
Vegetables		Compost/bins	
Fruit		Bonfire area	
Greenhouse		Boat/caravan standing	
Shed		Anything else	
Pond/pool			
Sandpit			

How much maintenance can you manage?	
Number/ages of children	
Pets	
Anything you do not want	

Certain features that you may want will affect the overall design of your garden far more than others. For example, the inclusion of space to park a boat or caravan, the position of a swimming pool or the provision of a large rock garden for the culture of alpines may provide a pivot around which the whole garden revolves or at least to which it must relate.

There are also personal considerations to take into account as you make your list. Ask yourself the following questions:

a How much time have I got?
b How much energy have I got?
c How much money do I want to spend?

The answers to these questions are vital to the success of your plans. It is better to plan and carry out a modest design for your garden than to overestimate your time, energy and money and run out of all three before you have finished. Bear in mind, though, that by having a design to work to you can spread all these factors over a considerable period, without losing track of the original concept.

WHAT HAVE YOU GOT IN YOUR GARDEN ALREADY?

To find this out you need to conduct a simple survey of the garden and draw up a sketch plan (or survey drawing). This must be done with care to produce an accurate basis for your design.

Measuring and mapping existing features

As with any job, the correct tools are essential. You will need the following: a long measuring tape (which can be hired if necessary); a clipboard; a few bamboo canes; a clean sheet of paper and a pencil.

● Go into your garden and on your sheet of paper draw your house, indicating the positions of doors and windows, as well as any other buildings such as a garage, greenhouse or shed. Mark in the approximate position of trees or planting (all planted areas including lawns) and with the latter include anything that is worth keeping. It is amazing how a seemingly insignificant shrub or small tree can provide the backbone or a focal point within a border or garden at a later date.

Now go on to measure your house and garden and instead of noting the distances between the end of a wall and a door, or between two windows, take running measurements. This quite simply involves fixing the tape at an appropriate point, using a cane as anchor if necessary, and unwinding it until you have reached the other side of the garden or the end of the tape, making sure you keep parallel with the wall. Now read off the distances in sequence and jot them down on your sketch plan. If the tape does not reach right the way across or down the garden, insert a cane at the end of the run, reel the tape in and use the cane as the starting point for a second set of measurements. Do not forget to show this 'change point' clearly on your plan. The sketch plan (see Figure 1.1) is later used to prepare a scale drawing (see Figure 1.2).

This first stage of your survey is very straighforward, particularly if the garden is rectangular with few additional features. Should any of the boundaries be set at an angle to the building or should you wish to plot the exact position of trees, shrubs or other features, you can use a different technique. In surveying terms it is called *triangulation*, which means fixing a point by three measurements taken as follows.

• Go out into your garden and choose a tree or shrub to plot. Run the tape from one corner of your house or garage, which you previously noted, to the tree and write down the measurement. Then move the tape to another known point which you have noted on your sketch plan

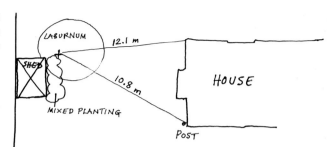

and repeat the operation (see Figure 1.3). When you come to transfer these measurements to a scale drawing (see Chapter 2, 'Designing your garden') you can use a pair of compasses to draw two arcs, with radii of the two measurements you noted, from the corresponding points involved. The point at which they intersect will mark the exact position of the tree or shrub (see Figure 1.4).

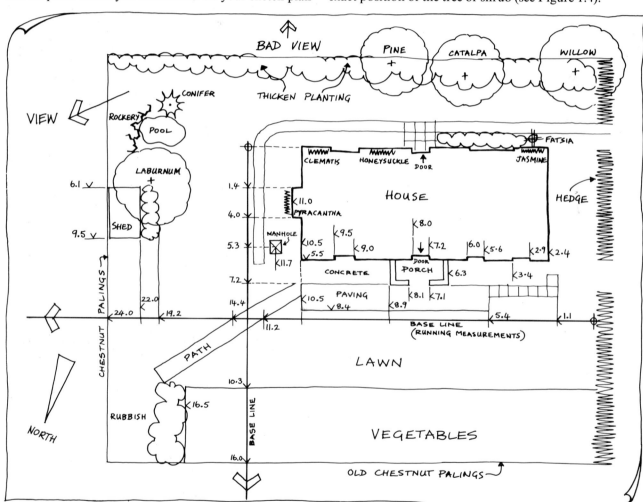

Figure 1.1 The survey drawing taken in the garden (above). It clearly shows the base lines and the running measurements taken. It also shows the other features within the garden. This survey covers only part of the plot; other drawings can be made to cover other areas. By doing this you can keep each drawing relatively simple and uncluttered.

Figure 1.2 The scale drawing taken from the survey (right). It is based on a grid, each square representing 1 m. The running measurements that were taken are indicated both across and down the drawing and all the features have been plotted accurately.

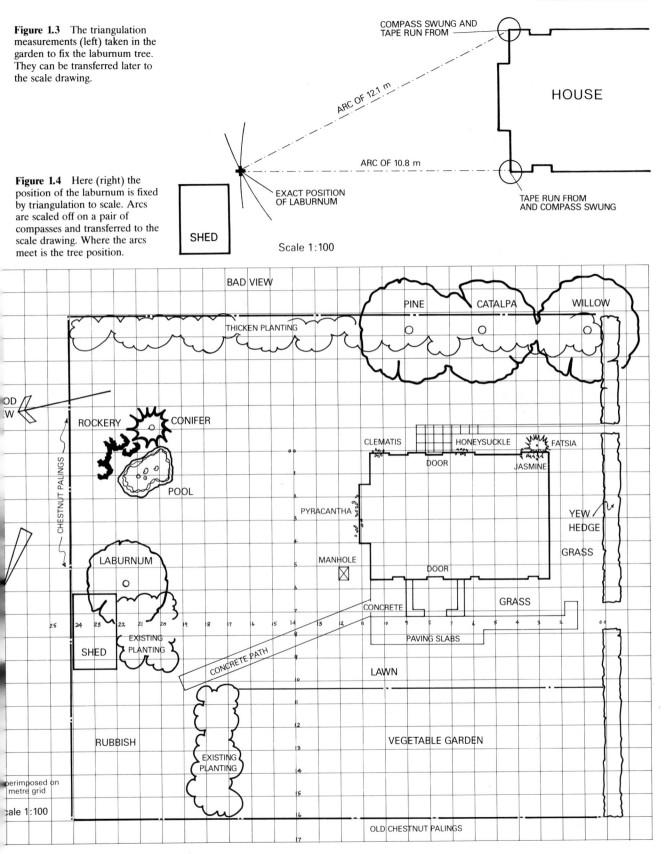

Figure 1.3 The triangulation measurements (left) taken in the garden to fix the laburnum tree. They can be transferred later to the scale drawing.

Figure 1.4 Here (right) the position of the laburnum is fixed by triangulation to scale. Arcs are scaled off on a pair of compasses and transferred to the scale drawing. Where the arcs meet is the tree position.

COMPASS SWUNG AND TAPE RUN FROM

ARC OF 12.1 m

ARC OF 10.8 m

HOUSE

EXACT POSITION OF LABURNUM

TAPE RUN FROM AND COMPASS SWUNG

SHED

Scale 1:100

BAD VIEW

PINE   CATALPA   WILLOW

THICKEN PLANTING

OD W

ROCKERY   CONIFER

CHESTNUT PALINGS

CLEMATIS   HONEYSUCKLE   FATSIA

DOOR   JASMINE

PYRACANTHA

POOL

YEW
HEDGE
GRASS

LABURNUM

MANHOLE

DOOR

GRASS

CONCRETE

25   24   23   22   21   20   19   8   17   6   15   14   13   2   1   0   9   8   7   6   5   4   3   2   1   0 0

SHED   EXISTING PLANTING

PAVING SLABS

CONCRETE PATH

LAWN

RUBBISH

EXISTING PLANTING

VEGETABLE GARDEN

perimposed on metre grid

cale 1:100

OLD CHESTNUT PALINGS

How can I measure a slope?

If your site is complicated by slopes that run in different directions or steep gradients that disappear around dog-legged boundaries and thick woodland, then it may be worth employing a surveyor with specialised equipment, paying his fee in the knowledge that the survey he gives you will be correct. You can also safely assume that this is precisely what professional landscape gardeners do. An involved survey is a job best left to experts. If, however, the slopes are not too steep and you feel that the changes of level could play an important part in your subsequent design, then check them yourself in one of the following ways:

a If your garden is terraced, remember that a course of brickwork is about 7.5 cm deep and you can use this measurement to assess drops.

b A far more precise method is to use homemade 'boning rods' (as shown in Figure 1.5). These are sharpened stakes with a 'T' piece nailed on the top. You will need about six of these. Drive in a short boning rod (A) at the top of the slope so that it projects about 30 cm above ground level. Place a long, straight-edged board on the rod and drive in a longer boning rod (B) further down the slope to support the other end. Make any adjustments to the second rod by placing a spirit level on top of the straight edge. The bubble should be dead centre. This now means that the two boning rods are horizontal. Look across the tops and place a third rod further down the slope and drive it in so that the three tops coincide. There will be no need to use the straight edge and spirit level again. If you have a steep slope it will be difficult to make boning rods long enough to

sight back to the starting point and in this case measure equal distances down the last two rods, nail on new cross-pieces and take sightings from these, continuing as before. To calculate the overall fall of ground add the height adjustments together and also add the *difference* in height from ground level to the top of the first rod and to the top of the last (see the example in Figure 1.5).

Now that your measurements are complete there are four other factors to take into consideration for your survey: views, shelter, soil, and the watertable. These will be considered in turn.

Views

Look around and ask yourself the following questions:

a Are there good or bad views that I can emphasise or screen?

b Am I overlooked by neighbouring upstairs windows, or houses on higher ground?

There are positive and negative aspects here. If you open a gap in an overgrown hedge a distant view can be drawn into your composition, providing a real focal point. Similarly, an open view of a landscape can often be made far more interesting if all of it is not seen at once. You can achieve this by planting, to provide a frame and added emphasis. Bad views can obviously be screened by walls, fences or planting, while the provision of a pergola (plant-covered walkway) or overhead beams (see Chapter 8, 'Features and furnishings') that run out from the building can be particularly useful in an urban situation to break the sight lines from surrounding buildings. The tradi-

Figure 1.5 Boning rods offer a simple means of measuring a bank or slope. The fall is calculated by taking the sum of the height adjustments and adding the difference in heights of the first and last rods from the ground.

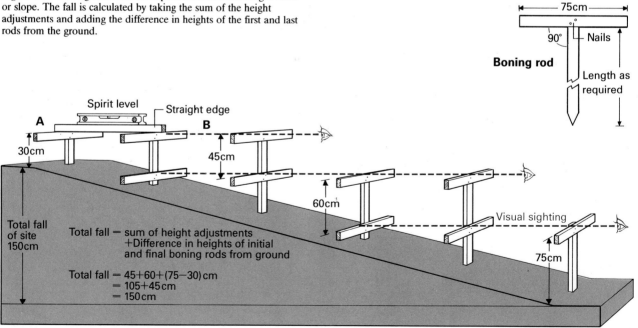

tional garden feature of a 'moon gate', which took the form of a circular hole through a boundary wall, can still be used today. Variations on this could take the form of large shutters that can be closed during inclement weather or when security is needed.

● Mark on your sketch plan any places where you can emphasise or block out views. (Chapter 4, 'Walls and fences', and Chapter 7, 'Plants and planting design', should help you decide how you might do this most effectively.)

Shelter

The amount of shelter in your garden is what really dictates the amount of time you can spend in it. Shelter, sun, shade and frost make up the elements of what is broadly termed the microclimate. The amount of light, wind and water affects the development of plants and consequently the position of large shrubs or trees modifies the lower-growing species in their vicinity. A south-facing slope, as opposed to flat ground, increases the amount of sunlight that plants receive; a north-facing slope has the reverse effect. It is also worth remembering that water reflects light, increasing the solar energy available in its locality. Aspect, or the position of the sun in relation to the garden, is a vital part of your survey and will determine not only what plants grow where, but the position of sitting areas, pools and many other features.

● Mark the position of north on your sketch plan.

Frost can be a real problem and is caused on clear nights by ground heat radiating away. Cloudy weather helps to reflect heat back to the ground, as do overhanging trees and large shrubs. The application of straw or sacking will also reduce the effects of frost. Frost pockets are simply low-lying areas, often at the bottom of a slope, in which cold air collects. The removal of a section of hedge or wall is usually enough to allow this to disperse and maintain a free passage of air.

● Mark on your sketch plan any modifications you can make to eliminate frost pockets.

Wind is perhaps the greatest problem, however, and the fact that this comes from a prevailing direction is greatly modified by the position of trees, planting and buildings. Buildings, in particular, can present real difficulties. Wind blowing at an oblique angle along a wall tends to accelerate, while wind coming at right angles is both forced up and turned under itself, to blow back the way it came, creating very turbulent conditions indeed. In both these instances you can position planting to deflect the full force of the wind before it reaches the building.

A solid wind-break creates turbulence on both sides which can do more harm than good. A slatted fence, pierced screen wall or light foliaged trees are far better, slowing the wind rather than forming a barrier, but the fact that they provide less privacy should also be taken into consideration.

● Mark on your sketch plan any places where fences or plants could be introduced to lessen wind problems. (See also Chapter 4, 'Walls and fences', and Chapter 7, 'Plants and planting design'.)

Soil

In structural terms the type of soil in your garden will make little difference, but the picture can be modified greatly when you consider planting, as the type of soil often determines what you can and cannot grow.

Soil comes in two broad layers: topsoil is fertile and supports plant growth; subsoil is infertile. The depth of both depends in part on the type of underlying rock and also on the forces of erosion. Some soils are quite different from the rock below and have been brought from elsewhere by glaciation or river action.

Topsoil is formed from subsoil and the basic rock below and is organically alive with bacteria, fungi and insects which live on vegetable debris, converting it into humus. Such an environment can be easily upset and if topsoil is compacted or becomes waterlogged for any length of time the structure is lost along with fertility. All this should be borne in mind when you move soil. The action of builders on new estates where topsoil is stripped or simply buried under subsoil and hardcore is totally irresponsible.

Is your soil heavy or light, clay or sandy?

Soil types can vary greatly from one garden or area to the next. These may be classified broadly into heavy or light, clay or sandy. Heavy, clay soils have small particles that tend to stick together. They are often fertile because minerals are washed away only slowly, but they are wet and slow to warm up. Sandy soils are made up from larger particles, drain quickly, with an equivalent loss of minerals, but warm up faster. Both extremes benefit from the addition of any organic matter, humus or compost, but bear in mind that perennial weeds should not be included in the latter category because they will not be killed by composting. The addition of these materials breaks down heavy soils and binds together lighter types. Drainage is improved in both cases. Peat is sold in vast quantities through garden centres and shops and its chief merit is as a soil conditioner to improve soil structure. It has no nutritional value but makes an excellent mulch that can help retain moisture.

To find out what kind of soil you have, take a trowel and collect a few samples from different parts of your garden. Wet the soil and rub it between your finger and thumb. How does it feel? This test will tell you whether your soil is made up of large or small particles.

– If the wetted soil sample feels sticky you have a clay soil.
– If it feels coarse and gritty you have a sandy soil.

Gardening books often talk of loam as being the perfect soil. This is approximately half way between sticky clays and porous sands with a well-balanced proportion of organic material. It is easy to work and drains well. Dark soils absorb solar energy more quickly than lighter-coloured ones, producing earlier crops. This was the reason why old gardeners kept soot on their allotments. It was used as a topdressing, or mixed with water, to darken the ground.

Is your soil chalky or acid?

Another important consideration is the acidity or alkalinity of a soil and this will certainly dictate what plants can be grown in a specific situation. Chalk or limestone in an area will almost always mean a high alkaline content, while a soil that has a high percentage of organic matter, peat in particular, will usually be acid. In basic terms a soil at either extreme needs applications of material from the other end of the scale; acid peat will help reduce alkalinity to a slight degree, while dressings of lime will reduce acidity.

The level of acidity or alkalinity is measured on a pH scale from 0 to 14, on which 7.0 is neutral. Numbers above this are alkaline and below are acid. Rhododendrons, azaleas and certain heathers grow well only in an acid soil and if you see these thriving in a locality they indicate soil acidity.

You can buy a simple kit to test the pH of your soil and this is a worthwhile exercise. Remember to take samples from different parts of the garden as the soil can vary from one part to another. As a final point it is not a good idea to try to grow plants from one soil type in another. You can spend vast sums making a chalky soil acid so that you can grow acid-loving plants, but the plain fact is that this seldom works and plants are rarely happy because the soil slowly reverts to type. By all means reduce extremes, but respect what grows naturally in an environment. This is one of the prime rules of design, and of common sense. The folly of planting rhododendrons on the South Downs should be obvious in both visual and cultural terms.

The watertable

The watertable is the level at which water stands above impervious rock. It can rise and fall in response to rainfall but it can also be affected by the erection of new buildings or by earth moving. A high watertable means stunted roots and poor development, while lack of water deprives plants of minerals in solution. Irrigation may help the latter, while drainage may be necessary to lower the watertable (see Chapter 3, 'Levels and drainage').

CHECKPOINT

Now that you have read this chapter you should have assessed what you want in your garden and what you have already. To check that you have understood the operations involved in doing this, answer the following questions.

1 What are the advantages of taking several months to list what you want in your garden? Try to think of at least two.
2 Which three personal considerations should you take into account when you list the features you want in your garden?
3 How do you take running measurements?
4 What is the best technique for plotting the positions of trees, shrubs and buildings, and how do you carry this out?
5 List two ways of measuring a slope.
6 How could you:
   a emphasise a good view;
   b block out a bad view?
7 What could you introduce into your garden to increase the solar energy available to a specific area?
8 How can you tell what type of soil you've got in your garden?
9 What happens if you try to grow plants suited to a soil type different from yours?
10 What happens to plants if the watertable in your garden is too high?

Check your answers and methods against the information given in the chapter.

CHAPTER TWO

Designing your garden

*Style/Materials/Colours/Preparing a site plan/Layout
Design/Garden shapes/Other design features
Checkpoint*

What does 'garden design' mean to you? Does it make you think of glossy magazine pictures you see in waiting rooms which you feel cannot possibly relate to your backyard, or moments of spontaneous inspiration by a designer which result in an ideal garden?

Design is often thought to be some kind of magic process which is unrelated to ordinary, everyday life. But that is not so. A good designer, apart from having a natural skill, relies on a combination of hard work and a well-tried set of rules that guide him or her to a sensible end result. Good design is not only simple and straightforward but, as was stressed in Chapter 1, reflects the personalities of those it serves, which is why no two gardens are identical.

So, *your* garden will reflect *your* personality. It will also take into account the advantages and limitations of your site and the information you gathered in Chapter 1. All these make up the bones of a most exciting proposition – the creation of a new environment for you and your family.

Before you get to grips with what goes where and how much space to give to various functions, you must first consider what overall style your garden should take.

STYLE

I have already touched on the incongruity of, say, rhododendrons on chalk downland or Cotswold stone used in the Pennines and to take this a stage further you need to recognise and respect local building patterns and the landscape in which they reside. There may be a very obvious theme. An old manor house set in sweeping lawns with fine cedars is not likely to engender yards of concrete paving, cantilevered steps or garish sunblinds, although none of these things would be unsuitable in the right context. Instead, you might think of brick paved terraces, a traditional stone balustrade, formal pools and softly planted borders. Conversely, such elements would almost certainly look of place with a crisp architectural building of glass and steel. Immediately, then, you can see that respect for surroundings is one of the prime design criteria.

You may be lucky enough to live in a house that has a very definite style which you can continue. However, most situations are not nearly as clear-cut as this. Many of us live in houses of nondescript style, which, although comfortable, have no particular image that can be projected outside. Even worse, there are vast numbers of new properties being built every year and most of these stand in completely featureless plots with no vegetation that could form a pivot or starting point for a design.

Having said that, there are still themes that you can develop – usually far more than are immediately apparent – for example, the use of various different materials and colours.

MATERIALS

Existing materials are often a good starting point. If your house is brick then a percentage of brick paving in a terrace or patio area will provide an immediate link between buiding and garden. You can reinforce this link by starting brick courses, or the edge of a paving pattern, from a salient point such as the corner of a building, a set of steps, the main door or a french window. Because the house is a dominant feature, raised beds, walls around a sitting area and even strong architectural planting will provide vertical emphasis that will balance and integrate inside and outside living areas.

Local building materials also play an important part. Yards of pre-cast concrete slabs look uncomfortable against a mellow Cotswold stone and it pays to look around your immediate town or village environment. Not only are local materials far cheaper than 'imported' ones, owing to soaring transport costs, but they look and feel correct. It is therefore well worth finding out about them.

But my house is built of concrete. What can I do?
In many ways you have the freest hand of all and as long as you keep your composition simple by limiting the number of materials you use, you can incorporate virtually anything – a slightly raised timber deck of neatly sawn planks, railway sleepers, concrete, brick, stone, cobbles or gravel (see Chapter 5, 'Hard landscape'). All will be suitable and all attractive. The perfect link is a continuation of flooring from inside to out, for example the old stone flags of a farmhouse running out to a terrace, the crisp lines of slate from a basement studio or the reassuring scale of frost-proof tiles from a penthouse kitchen on to a roof garden. These are delicious extremes but the lesson remains the same even on a far more domestic scale.

COLOURS

If you have a garden wall that abuts your house you have an immediate opportunity to extend the colour scheme from an adjoining wall inside, using a simple colour wash. The colours of plants in tubs, pots or anything else can make the transition between inside and out almost incidental and this is one area where the ubiquitous 'patio door' has been of immense help in allowing light, colour, views, sound and, when open, fragrance to flow together. Remember that there is far more to a garden than visual appeal. All the senses are involved and the greater their collective stimulation the better the end result.

PREPARING A SITE PLAN

By now you are aware of not only the inherent characteristics of your site but also your collective needs and the overall style you wish to adopt. At last it is time actually to put pencil to paper and prepare a site plan to scale from the measurements you have taken already.

For this you will need squared graph paper and a pair of compasses. On your graph paper let one or a number of squares represent 1 metre (or 1 foot). For a garden of average size the scale of 1:100 (10 mm:1 m) is suitable, while for a small garden you can use 1:50 (20 mm:1 m).

• To prepare a scale drawing it is easiest to work on tracing paper over graph paper.

a Attach the sheet of graph paper to a smooth, firm board (a drawing board is ideal) using drafting tape or Sellotape.

b Place the tracing paper over the top and stick this down in a similar way.

c Choose your scale; let us assume that each square on the graph paper represents 1 metre in the garden.

d Refer to your survey drawing and transfer the running measurements you took in the garden to the scale drawing. By doing this the pattern of house and boundaries will be built up.

e Where triangulation for, say, a tree is involved use the following technique. Check the survey drawing and ascertain the two known points that were used to run the tape out to the tree. Mark these on the scale drawing. Check the distance from the first to the tree and extend your compasses to scale accordingly. Place the compass point in the correct position and draw an arc. Repeat the operation for the second measurement. The point at which they intersect will mark the exact position of the tree.

f When all your measurements have been transferred you can go over the pencil with a drawing pen in ink, thus making a permanent record. Finally rub out the pencil.

You have now transferred everything from your sketch plan: the measurements you have taken; the position of trees, shrubs and manhole covers; the position of views and any places where you want to emphasise or block

them out; prevailing winds and any places where screening is necessary; modifications you can make to eliminate frost pockets; and most important the north point, or where the sun shines in relation to your garden, and areas of shade. You can pencil in changes of level, if applicable, along with the positions of banks and types of boundary.

Once you have completed your scale drawing, either take lots of photocopies or make copies using tracing paper. If you work on the original you will soon reduce it to a meaningless jumble of lines, rubbings out and confusion, – the last thing you want at this stage!

Now you are ready to think about the layout of your garden.

LAYOUT

• Look at the list you made of what you want in your garden. Place the items in order of importance, writing (1) against the most important feature, (2) against the next, and so on. On your plan, rough in or allocate areas for separate functions, giving the most space to the features with lower numbers, i.e. those you consider most important (see Figure 2.1). As you do this keep the following points in mind:

a Think carefully about the location of each feature. For example, if you want a terrace for sitting, dining and entertaining, this would probably be best located abutting your house, provided there is adequate shelter and sun in that area. For help with siting other features see Chapter 8, 'Features and furnishings'.

b Consider how various features on your list might relate to one another; for example, dustbins, oil tank and fuel store could be housed in a single structure, while shed, greenhouse and compost may also form an integral group. As most gardens are small and the components many, try to draw the related elements together to produce the most restful end result.

c Front and back gardens are often considered as separate entities, but with more enlightened building styles a garden can flow far more naturally around the house and there is no need, provided the site characteristics are suitable, for vegetables to be at the rear. Bins, too, could be in the front garden, suitably screened, while a raised pool or bed could be perfect by the front door, leading both feet and eye in the required direction.

d Sun and wind are prime considerations in the positioning of features. You will have no desire to sit in a shady, draughty corner, and many plants certainly demand sun. You can easily provide shelter by erecting a wall or screen, so rough in the positions of this if it is needed.

e Noise is often a problem these days, perhaps from a busy road or adjoining playground. A gently contoured bank, planted with a combination of shrubs and trees, will not only give a soft backdrop but also soak up a surprising level of noise.

It is unlikely that your first few rough plans will be anything like the finished pattern, but priorities and areas will be emerging. Never throw these first ideas away; by comparing them you can steadily improve the layout. There is a saying in the landscape profession about not crystallising too soon. This is sound advice. Take your time, and remember that although a trained designer may have experience on his side, you have on your side a familiarity with any problems and intimate knowledge of what you need.

The next step is to consider how you can turn your rough ideas into a pleasing design.

Figure 2.1 In this sketch plan of the original garden the required priorities of the finished design have been 'roughed in'. This information has been gathered from our checklist and survey.

DESIGN

In basic terms design is the moulding of single ideas and features into a sensible, and invariably simple, whole. Few good designs are complicated and none are fussy. Neither do they just happen. They are, if you like, calculated pattern-making to suit very particular requirements.

Simplicity imposes constraint and this in turn depends on a sequence of steps that give the entire composition continuity.

If you assume that your house is the starting point of your design it will make sense to plan the areas that adjoin the building in an 'architectural or structured way' to reinforce the link between house and garden. The further away you get, the softer and looser your composition can be, providing a feeling of space and movement that leads

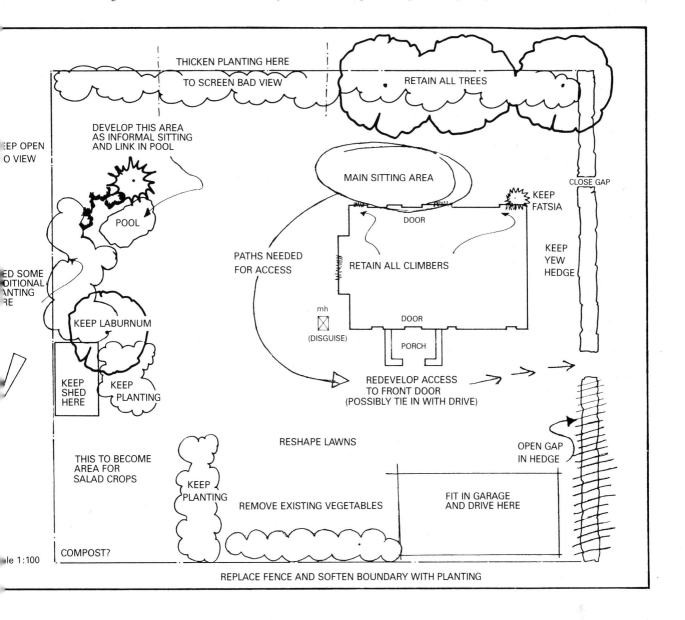

the eye away from rectangular boundaries. This being the case, you should think of modular shapes and materials close to the house. The all-too-frequent use of crazy paving for a terrace is unsound: all those conflicting lines and joints clash with the cleaner lines of the building. Crazy paving used in the further parts of the garden for an informal sitting area, softened by grass and planting, is altogether more sensible.

Formal and informal gardens

All too often you hear of formal and informal gardens, as if these were the only two available designs. The fact of the matter is that a formal garden relies on symmetry (one side mirrors the other) and this either reflects the architecture of a building or is alternatively an entirely separate 'set piece', possibly contained by walls and taking the form of a rose or herb garden. The symmetry of a formal garden is inevitably a static affair but when properly used can be most effective, if rather impractical in a family setting.

Asymmetry, on the other hand, is rather different and altogether more flexible. The basis of an asymmetric design is balance rather than reflection, and can be quite simply demonstrated by the position of heavy and light weights on either side of a fulcrum (see Figure 2.2). Translated into garden terms it means that a composition can be balanced by the juxtaposition of various features; for example, a large paved area on one side of the garden may be countered by a sweep of lawn or group of trees on the other; a number of smaller, interlocking shapes in one area may add up to a single bold pattern elsewhere. This feeling of proportion and rightness is paramount to garden and landscape design.

Making a model of your garden

Many people find it difficult to visualise from a plan what the garden will look like. The reason for this is that the plan is two-dimensional while, of course, the garden is in three dimensions. You can overcome this by making a three-dimensional model of your garden. For a simple model you will need: a base board of stiff card; thinner card that can be cut out to form cubes and trees; Sellotape or glue; felt tip pens; rubbers; pencils.

● Then proceed to make your model as follows:

a Transfer your rough plan to a sheet of cardboard. It is important that this is drawn to scale.

b If the garden slopes and you have, say, a patio raised above the rest of the garden, cut this shape out from a piece of thinner card, attach flaps and glue or stick it in place at a corresponding height.

c Colour the slabs grey or whatever colour is applicable to simulate the end result.

d Colour in the lawn, preferably green.

e Indicate the planted areas with cubes to indicate their *mass* rather than trying to show specific shrubs.

f Make cardboard trees and stick them in position.

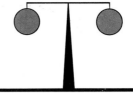

Symmetrical

Figure 2.2 Symmetry and asymmetry can be shown simply as weights balanced on either side of a fulcrum. In the illustration above, both weights are identical and are positioned equally on either side of the fulcrum (symmetrical). Below, the weights are unequal and positioned at different points (asymmetrical), but both examples balance.

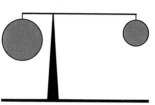

Asymmetrical

Figure 2.3 The finished design of the garden, incorporating all the features originally requested. The garden is an awkward shape but the pattern of lawn and planting ties the various elements together. There is now ample room for sitting and dining, in a combination of neat pre-cast concrete slabs and brick. The pine has become host to a built-in seat, and the herbs interlock with this to form an interesting composition. A path leads across to the informal sitting area that benefits from the good view, while stepping stones draw the pool and conifer into the composition. The salad crops fit neatly into the corner, and the new garage and drive provide ample parking space. As a final feature, that awkward strip at the side of the house has been floored with ground cover, and overhead beams frame the walkway.

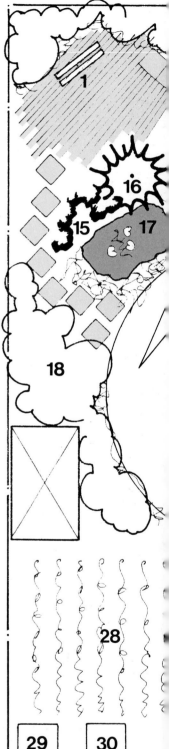

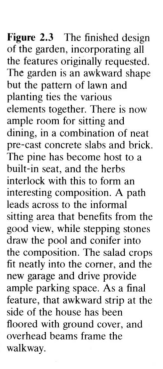

Scale 1:100

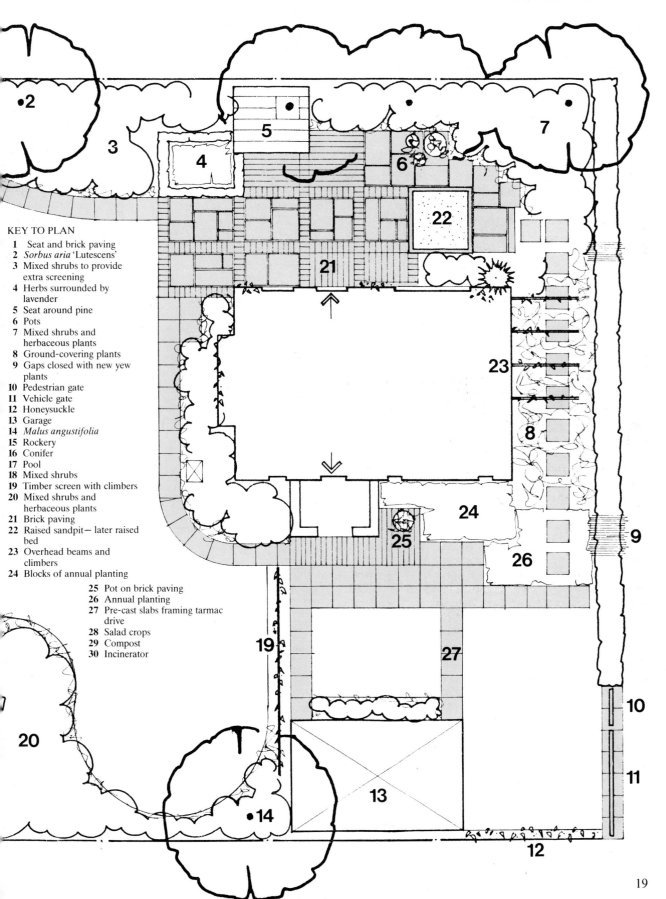

KEY TO PLAN

1 Seat and brick paving
2 *Sorbus aria* 'Lutescens'
3 Mixed shrubs to provide extra screening
4 Herbs surrounded by lavender
5 Seat around pine
6 Pots
7 Mixed shrubs and herbaceous plants
8 Ground-covering plants
9 Gaps closed with new yew plants
10 Pedestrian gate
11 Vehicle gate
12 Honeysuckle
13 Garage
14 *Malus angustifolia*
15 Rockery
16 Conifer
17 Pool
18 Mixed shrubs
19 Timber screen with climbers
20 Mixed shrubs and herbaceous plants
21 Brick paving
22 Raised sandpit— later raised bed
23 Overhead beams and climbers
24 Blocks of annual planting
25 Pot on brick paving
26 Annual planting
27 Pre-cast slabs framing tarmac drive
28 Salad crops
29 Compost
30 Incinerator

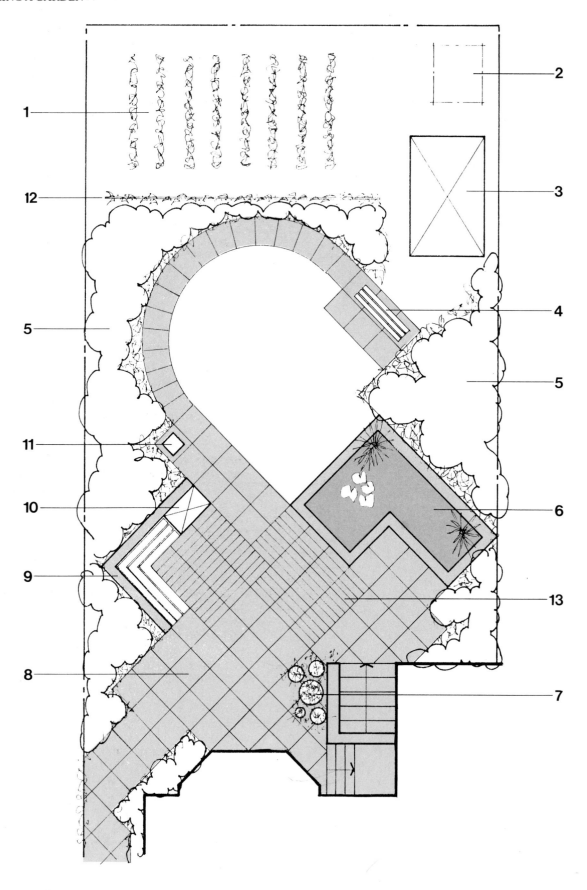

1

2

12

3

5

4

5

11

10

6

9

13

8

7

Alternatively, stick a pencil in a rubber, fix a circle of cardboard to represent foliage and move the whole thing about at random to see where a tree would best be planted.

g If you have children and cannot, or do not want to, build the model yourself, ask them: they are excellent at this sort of thing and teachers love such projects.

Once you have done this the difference between plan and elevation will become apparent. Curves and angles viewed from ground level look far tighter than on a drawing. Hold your model up to your eye and look across it. This will give you a pretty good idea of what the end result will look like.

Where can I find ideas for my garden design?

Look for inspiration in the design of fabrics, wallpapers and carpets. Many of these patterns adapt extremely well to a garden ground plan (see below) as do abstract paintings by such artists as Mondrian and Klee.

Making a ground plan

The ground plan that you work out is in real terms the 'design' and incorporates all the information you have gathered, together with the criteria you need to bring the garden alive.

The materials you need to do this are a copy of the scale drawing on tracing paper, pencils and a rubber, a ruler or set square and the grid you used to prepare the scale drawing.

● The grid used to prepare the scale drawing can be used to prepare the ground plan. Take one of the copies of your scale drawing previously made on tracing paper and lay this over the grid, using the same metric or imperial scale as you did in preparing the site plan.

You have seen that it can be useful to start a design from a corner of a building or a set of french windows. In a terrace area you can work out the pattern of paving over the grid: for example, two squares on the grid might represent one paving slab. You can rough in the proportions of material, say brick paving and pre-cast concrete slabs, as well as specific features such as built-in seating, a barbecue and overhead beams (see Figure 2.3).

Figure 2.4 In this garden the whole paving pattern has been turned at an angle of 45°, picking up the line of the bay window and forming a strong link between house and garden. A seat and barbecue are practical features and the path sweeps round to the seat, which acts as a focal point. The vegetables are neatly screened and planting softens the boundaries.

KEY TO PLAN

1	Vegetables	7 Pots
2	Compost	8 Pre-cast slabs
3	Shed	9 Wall at about 105 cm
4	Seat	10 Barbecue with seat to left
5	Mixed planting	11 Statue
6	Raised pool	12 Espalier fruit as screen
		13 Brick paving

Sometimes you can turn the whole design at an angle to the house (see Figure 2.4). This immediately leads the eye away from the overpowering shape of rectangular boundaries. Also, remember that diagonal lines are the longest distance across a rectangle because you may be able to use them to create a feeling of greater space.

Build up the garden pattern roughly to start with, allocating space for the various components as I have already suggested. Gradually such positions can be made firm and honed down to a clean, crisp design that works in both visual and practical terms.

GARDEN SHAPES

Gardens can be square, narrow, wide, long, triangular, have dog-legs and so on. Your requirements will have to be fitted into your plot but there are certain techniques that can both enhance the end result and also make life a lot easier for you.

Long and narrow

Train journeys can be enlightening, particularly when passing through the suburbs of a city. Here you have a bird's eye view of countless gardens and by far the most common is that long, narrow shape that recedes into the distance. All too often you see the classic mistake: a path down the middle, echoed by the washing line, narrow borders along each side and usually vegetables or rubbish at the bottom. All this does is emphasise the shape, in much the same way as a pin-striped suit does on a thin man. Such a garden, however, is the perfect shape for subdivision into 'rooms', each one having a separate theme and subsequently breaking the length into a number of far more manageable areas (see Figure 2.5).

A typical example might have a terrace close to the house, partially enclosed by raised beds or built-in seating. A lawn of roughly square proportions, softened by planting, might follow, while the third room, screened, perhaps, by a hedge or a pierced wall, might be given over to vegetables, shed or greenhouse. The final area at the bottom of the garden could be floored with rougher grass, naturalised with bulbs and given over to fruit trees and the children's swing. All these sections could be interchangeable. There is nothing shameful about a welltended allotment, and this, combined with herbs and flowers for cutting, could play a dominant role, perhaps next to the house.

Instead of a path running down the middle, why not start it on one side of the terrace and lead it down the garden in a series of right angles, again leading feet and eye *across* rather than down the space? In such a garden the rooms could all be rectangular, or of different shapes. Add to this the suggestion of using a different type of colour of planting in each area and you turn a drab prospect into a positive feast of possibilities. Wings of planting, or hedges, can extend across a garden, overlapping and allowing the path to slide between. Not only does this create an air of mystery as the path disappears, but it also forms a 'tension point', where a view is restricted before bursting out into another room.

The use of interlocking rectangles and blocks of planting can also be used to good effect in a wide, short front garden (see Figure 2.6).

Figure 2.6 In a particularly awkward front garden the drive and pedestrian access have been combined and the ground plan is built up from a series of interlocking rectangles, based on an abstract pattern. Planting softens the garden and an area of gravel, boulders and ground cover provides a Japanese influence.

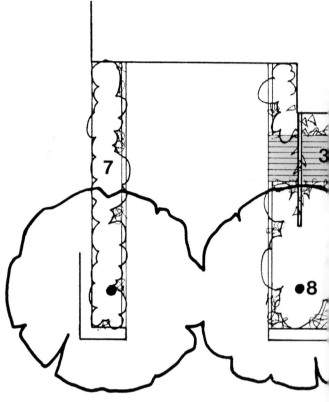

KEY TO PLAN

 1 Raised bed for bulbs and annuals
 2 Mixed shrubs and climbers
 3 Overhead beams and climbers
 4 Pots
 5 Statue
 6 Brick paving
 7 Mixed planting
 8 2 *Sorbus aucuparia*
 9 1 *Prunus communis*
10 Mixed shrubs and herbaceous plants
11 Roses surrounded by clipped box hedging
12 Seat
13 Roses surrounded by clipped box hedging
14 Boulders, planting and gravel
15 Mixed shrubs

Figure 2.5 The design for my own garden, a typical long, narrow plot that seems to go on forever. You can see how it has been broken down into separate areas or 'rooms'. Closest to the house is the main dining and sitting area, using old stable pavers that were already on site, together with square pre-cast concrete slabs. A seat surrounds a fine old holly tree and a small raised pool gives emphasis to one side. The garden has a gentle slope and broad steps drop down to each level. The path is kept on one side to increase the apparent width and then turns across the space before dropping down to the lowest lawn. By using this pattern we have created a series of far more manageable spaces.

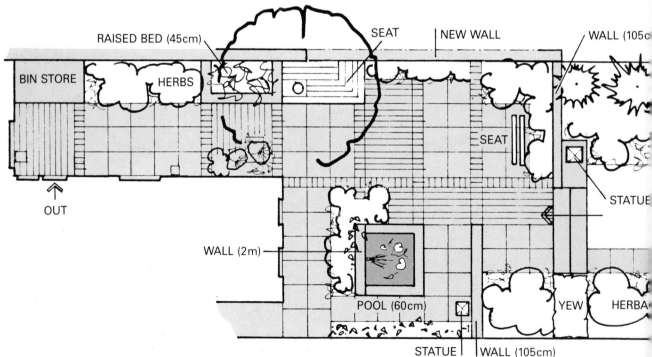

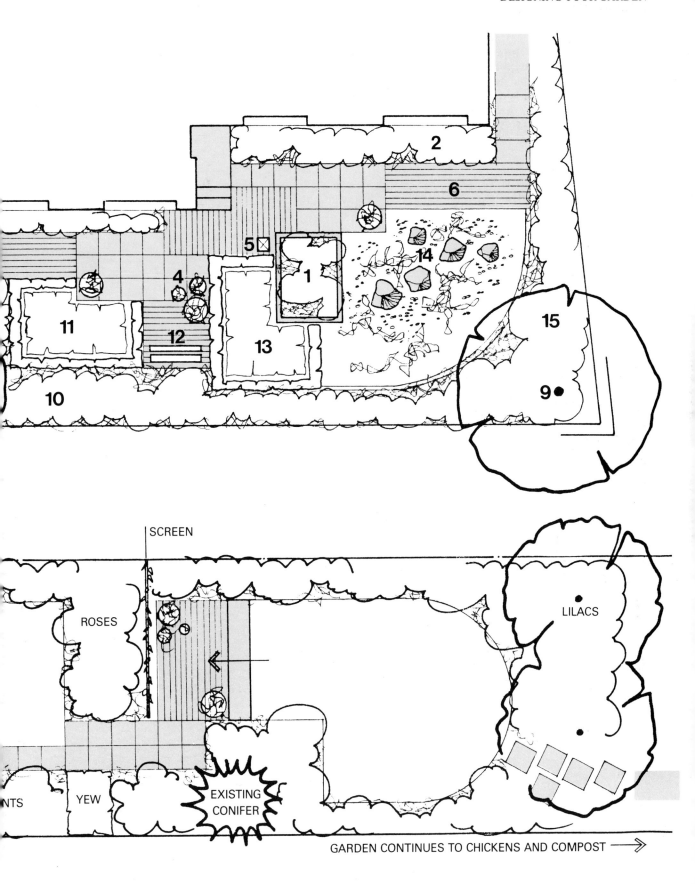

2

6

5

1

14

4

12

11

13

10

15

9

SCREEN

ROSES

LILACS

NTS YEW

EXISTING
CONIFER

GARDEN CONTINUES TO CHICKENS AND COMPOST ⟶

Dog-leg

Dog-leg gardens, of the sort that disappear round the side of a house, are also common and here, all too frequently, the action is concentrated in one half, the other becoming a forgotten and awkward corner. A circular pattern, or one that is built up from a series of strong, flowing curves, can draw the two halves together, providing a real feeling of continuity.

Square

A perfectly square plot is perhaps the most difficult shape of all; the others have at least got inherent movement in a particular direction. If there is a view out of the garden

Figure 2.7 This tiny garden has a fine view. The boundary fence has therefore been kept to a low post-and-rail type that could be removed entirely. Courses of brick tie the composition together and the paving has been emphasised by using wide joints. This is a simple design, as the best should be. See how the courses of brick run off the edge of the existing steps and link into the new garden features.

GOOD VIEW

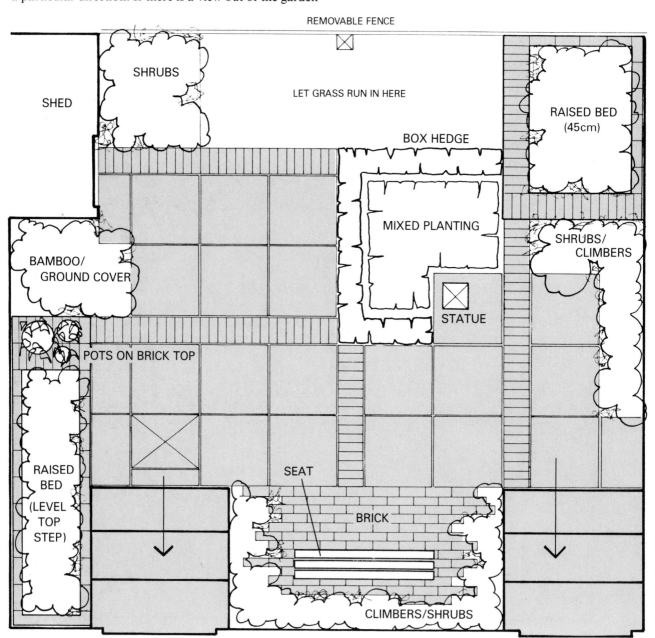

REMOVABLE FENCE

SHRUBS

SHED

LET GRASS RUN IN HERE

RAISED BED (45cm)

BOX HEDGE

MIXED PLANTING

BAMBOO/ GROUND COVER

SHRUBS/ CLIMBERS

STATUE

POTS ON BRICK TOP

RAISED BED (LEVEL TOP STEP)

SEAT

BRICK

CLIMBERS/SHRUBS

the problem is simplified, planting and the general pattern leading the eye and detracting from the basic shape (see Figure 2.7). If, however, there is nothing but four walls the pattern may have to turn in upon itself (see Figure 2.8), using curves or a composition of rectangles (see Figure 2.9) that build up a montage of different surfaces. Here, and in many other garden designs (see Figure 2.10), a focal point can be of enormous help. An old park bench positioned on a diagonal sight line, a sundial, statue or group of pots, or a carefully sited tree will all emphasise a particular direction. Remember, though, that such eye-catchers – and this includes conifers – are very much the

punctuation marks of a garden. Use them carefully, otherwise you will end up with an incomprehensible muddle.

● Using the above information, mark on your plan the pattern of shapes you will introduce into your garden to modify the overall shape.

Figure 2.8 This tiny courtyard garden was surrounded by walls and bad views. Here the design turns in upon itself to focus on a stone sundial. In this case the lawn is purely decorative, softening the hard landscape of old York stone and brick paving. Bins are housed in a neat store, while planting forms an envelope wrapping the garden in foliage.

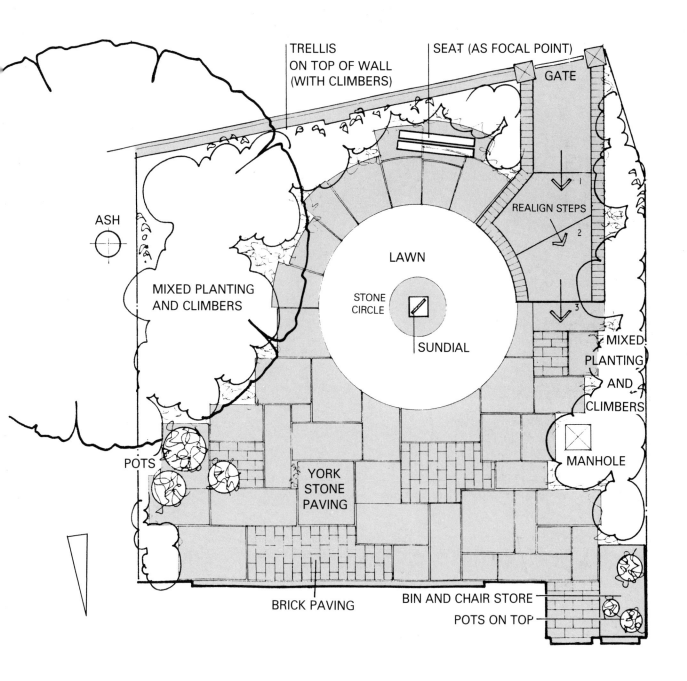

TRELLIS
ON TOP OF WALL
(WITH CLIMBERS)

SEAT (AS FOCAL POINT)

GATE

ASH

MIXED PLANTING
AND CLIMBERS

REALIGN STEPS

LAWN

STONE
CIRCLE

SUNDIAL

MIXED
PLANTING
AND
CLIMBERS

POTS

YORK
STONE
PAVING

MANHOLE

BRICK PAVING

BIN AND CHAIR STORE

POTS ON TOP

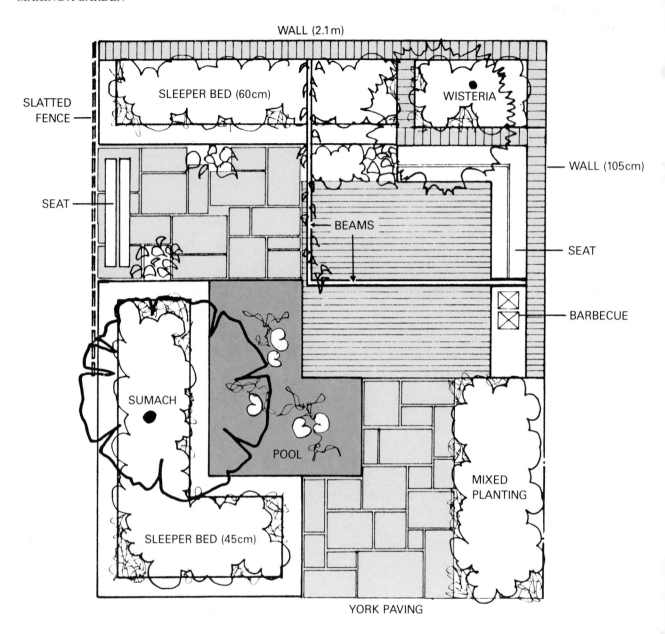

WALL (2.1 m)

SLATTED FENCE

SLEEPER BED (60 cm)

WISTERIA

WALL (105 cm)

SEAT

BEAMS

SEAT

BARBECUE

SUMACH

POOL

MIXED PLANTING

SLEEPER BED (45 cm)

YORK PAVING

OTHER DESIGN FEATURES

There are several other factors, common to all gardens, that you should take into account as you plan your design.

Curves

While straight lines are just that, curved patterns are different altogether. One of the curses of the English garden is very often its basic lack of purpose. Borders take on serpentine wiggles, paths wander aimlessly about. All this becomes even less positive when softened by age and planting. When you draw up a plan, and curves are called for, use a pair of compasses and do a proper job, sweeping

Figure 2.9 Here a courtyard garden underlines the fact that rectangles can be successfully used in a restricted area. This is an abstract pattern, built up from brick paving, York stone, water and raised beds constructed from railway sleepers.

one radius into the next. When you lay this out on the ground the result will show a strength of purpose that creates a perfect foil for foliage, tumbling and modifying the outline. In addition, curves need to go somewhere, either leading the eye to a focal point or linking shapes together (see Figure 2.11). Something that dives off into a fence or fades into oblivion really does nothing for the overall pattern.

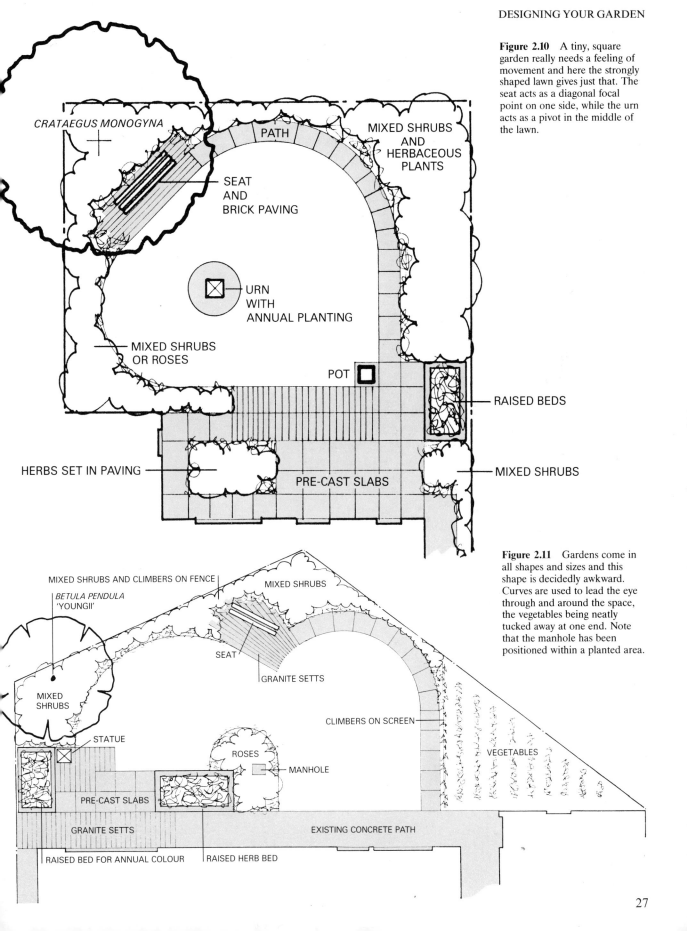

Figure 2.10 A tiny, square garden really needs a feeling of movement and here the strongly shaped lawn gives just that. The seat acts as a diagonal focal point on one side, while the urn acts as a pivot in the middle of the lawn.

CRATAEGUS MONOGYNA

PATH

MIXED SHRUBS AND HERBACEOUS PLANTS

SEAT AND BRICK PAVING

URN WITH ANNUAL PLANTING

MIXED SHRUBS OR ROSES

POT

RAISED BEDS

HERBS SET IN PAVING

PRE-CAST SLABS

MIXED SHRUBS

Figure 2.11 Gardens come in all shapes and sizes and this shape is decidedly awkward. Curves are used to lead the eye through and around the space, the vegetables being neatly tucked away at one end. Note that the manhole has been positioned within a planted area.

MIXED SHRUBS AND CLIMBERS ON FENCE

MIXED SHRUBS

BETULA PENDULA 'YOUNGII'

SEAT

GRANITE SETTS

MIXED SHRUBS

CLIMBERS ON SCREEN

STATUE

ROSES

MANHOLE

VEGETABLES

PRE-CAST SLABS

GRANITE SETTS

EXISTING CONCRETE PATH

RAISED BED FOR ANNUAL COLOUR

RAISED HERB BED

27

Figures 2.12, 2.13 and 2.14 are
three designs for an identical
plot and prove how different
gardens can be within a set
framework. The only feature
common to all three is the old
apple tree at the bottom.

Figure 2.12 This is a simple
pattern that allows ample space
for play and dining close to the
house. The path allows access
for wheeled toys; shed, salad
crops and slide fit in an area of
rougher grass under the tree.
The terrace paving is a
combination of pre-cast slabs
and concrete kerbs, the latter
being laid flat.

KEY TO PLAN

  1 Shed
  2 Slide
  3 Apple tree
  4 Salad crops
  5 Compost
  6 Screen hedge of beech
  7 Mixed shrubs and
     herbaceous plants
  8 Seat
  9 Mixed planting
 10 *Cercis siliquastrum*
 11 Pots
 12 Herbs surrounded by
     lavender
 13 Screen with climbers
 14 Raised sandpit
 15 Kerb edges laid flat
 16 Mixed planting
 17 Rotary drier
 18 Kerb edges
 19 Mixed planting

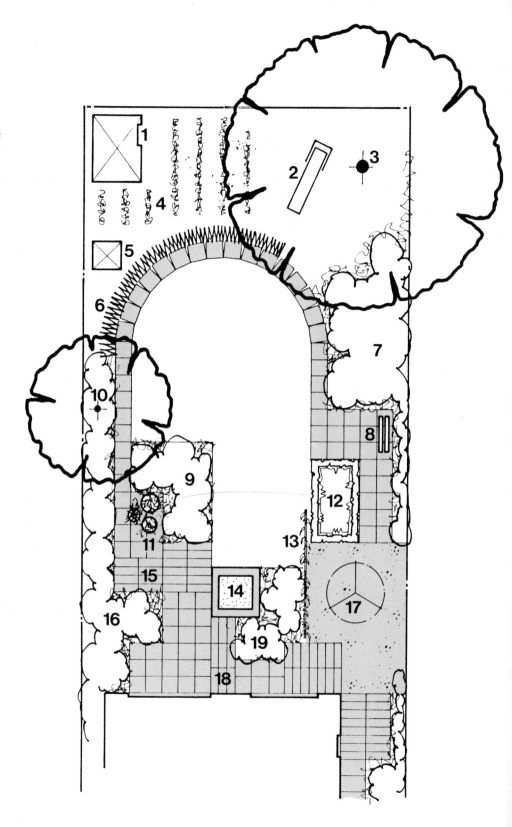

Figure 2.13 This is an altogether more fluid pattern, the design being turned at an angle to the house. The sitting area is a combination of engineering brick and brushed concrete. The seat and barbecue are contained by a wall 105 cm high and this continues as a wide wall, leading round to the pool. A path leads diagonally past the area of ground cover, planting and boulders, terminating at the brick paved sitting area under the tree.

KEY TO PLAN

1 Incinerator
2 Compost
3 Gate to back lane
4 Seat around apple
5 Mixed shrubs and herbaceous plants
6 Mixed shrubs
7 Statue
8 Brick paving
9 Boulders
10 Wall at 105 cm with spout into pool
11 2 *Rhus typhina* 'Laciniata'
12 Mixed planting
13 Pot
14 Seat
15 Mixed shrubs
16 Wall at 105 cm
17 Seat and barbecue
18 Pots
19 Brick paving (engineering brick with shiny surface)
20 Brushed concrete
21 Brick wall 45 cm high
22 Overhead beams and climbers spanning side passage

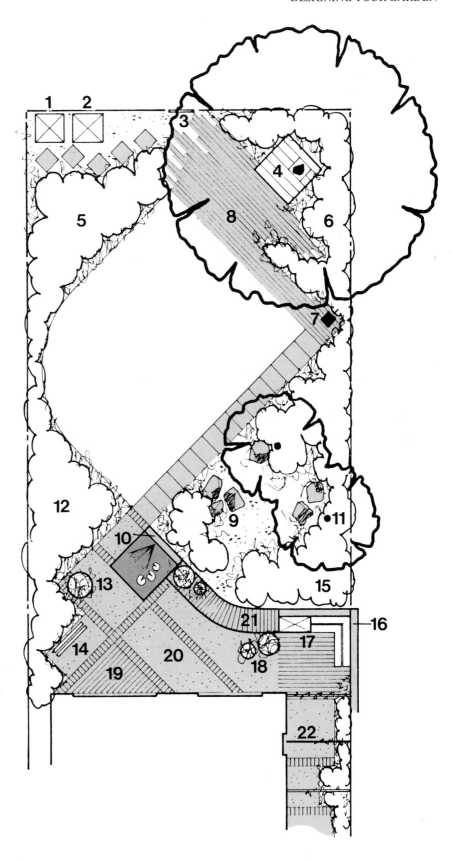

Figure 2.14 A traditional pattern built up from a rectangular grid. This is a garden that one needs to go 'through', one area leading to another, the pool being crossed by stepping stones. The lawns are on slightly different levels, linked by a brick step, while natural stone paving is used in conjunction with brick for the terrace.

KEY TO PLAN

 1 Vegetables
 2 Apple tree
 3 Compost
 4 Incinerator
 5 Greenhouse
 6 Seat
 7 Espalier fruit as screen
 8 Frames
 9 Yew hedge 1.5 m high
10 Raised bed
11 *Malus* 'Profusion'
12 Pot
13 Raised bed
14 Herbs surrounded by lavender
15 Lawn
16 Yew hedge 105 cm high
17 Mixed shrubs and herbaceous plants
18 Roses
19 Statue
20 Brick paving
21 Stepping stones through ground cover

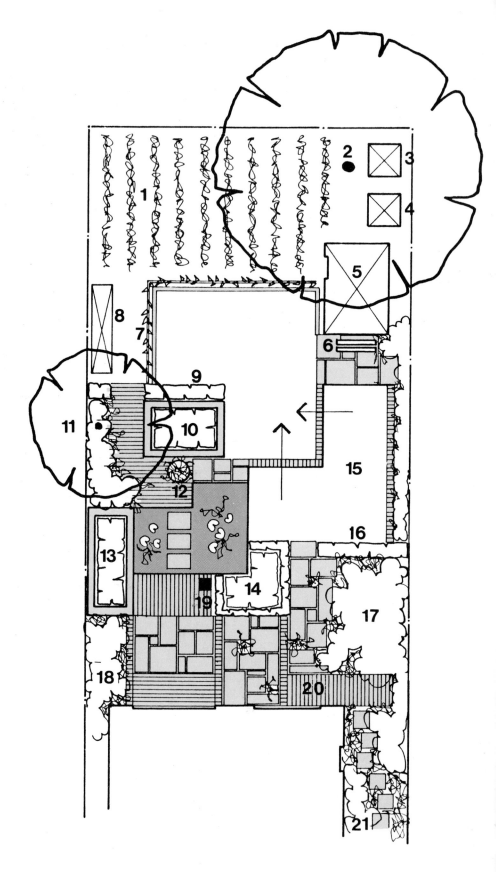

Light and shade

In countries where the light is stronger than in Britain, the interplay of light and shade is an integral part of garden design. The great Italian Renaissance gardens used a framework of clipped hedges and trees, so that by passing from pools of shadow into broad daylight another dimension was created. Our own light is softer but still strong enough to play an important part in design and the shadow cast by a tree can in itself create the transition between one area and another, while a pergola or arbour forms a darker, cooler area that can be most attractive during hot weather.

Levels

Changes of level in a garden can be either a hindrance or a help. In financial terms they can be expensive, as it is a costly business to build retaining walls and steps to separate different levels. On the positive side they can add immeasurably to the inherent interest of a design. They can be handled in a number of ways but it is worth bearing in mind that the creation of too many levels in a small garden can become 'fussy'. If falls are not great it may be best to work with them, allowing a garden to flow down and around a bank using planting to counterbalance a cross-fall.

In general, use the rules I have already set, keeping an architectural theme of beds and retaining walls close to the building and grading away into informality. The materials used for walling should again respect and reinforce the ground plan and the adjoining buildings. Such walls become almost incidental when softened by planting that can tumble from one level to another.

In a perfectly flat garden you can introduce interest by making changes in level, either by adding raised beds or by the cut-and-fill technique where soil is removed from one point and built up in another. When you do this, however, remember to stack the topsoil separately for re-use and also be aware that you may alter the drainage patterns by coming closer to the watertable. (For more information about levels and drainage see Chapter 3.)

Planting

Planting is covered in Chapter 7, but it is worth underlining here that this is the third dimension of garden design, providing shelter, screening, vertical emphasis as well as colour and interest through the year. The importance of trees, as pivots to a design, as focal points, or simply to cast shade in a certain position, should always be remembered and used to the best possible advantage. In the initial design stage planting is really concerned with building up the garden framework. In other words, think of plants as groups or sweeps of material rather than individual specimens; the selection of detailed varieties can come later on.

Figures 2.12, 2.13 and 2.14, showing three different designs for an identical plot, will give you some idea of the design possibilities open to you, bearing in mind the personalities and requirements of the families using them. In the final analysis the success of your design will depend on how well you have done your homework but, as I pointed out in Chapter 1, cost will undoubtedly play a vital role. It will be of little use preparing an exotic scheme with expensive materials if your budget will limit its implementation. On the other hand, the preparation of a design will allow work to be carried out in stages, perhaps over a number of years, in the safe knowledge that the original plan will remain intact.

CHECKPOINT

Now that you have read this chapter you should have decided what overall style your garden will take and what materials or colours you will use to develop a theme. You should have prepared several copies of a site plan on which to rough out your layout ideas, and used a ground plan to try out your design ideas, perhaps inspired by a fabric or wallpaper pattern and taking into account the shape of your garden and other inherent factors.

To check that you have understood these processes fully, answer the following questions.

1. Walk around your local area and look for good and bad examples of garden design. Have local building patterns and landscape been taken into account? Have appropriate materials been used which blend with the houses?
2. If you live in a brick house how could you link it to your garden?
3. What scale would you use for the site plan of a small garden?
4. How could you shield your garden from the noise of a nearby road?
5. Which is more suitable for a small garden, a symmetric or an asymmetric design?
6. How do you prepare a grid for a ground plan?
7. What design technique could you use to break up a long, narrow garden?
8. How can you draw together the two halves of a dog-leg garden?
9. Why should you avoid introducing too many levels into a small garden?
10. What are three functions of plants and trees in a garden design?

Check your answers against the information given in the chapter.

CHAPTER THREE

Levels and drainage

Effects of different levels/Creating different levels
Drainage/Checkpoint

EFFECTS OF DIFFERENT LEVELS

Why introduce different levels?

As you saw in Chapter 2, different levels can be used in a garden either to screen out an ugly view, to absorb noise, or quite simply to add interest to a completely flat garden. However, the introduction of different levels also has four other effects:

a A slope *up* from the house foreshortens the view, making the garden appear smaller than it is; a slope *down* from the house does the reverse and creates a feeling of distance. These are obviously very important points to remember when you are designing your garden.

b Slopes such as these, unless of the gentlest gradient, tend to produce a feeling of instability, which, in extreme cases may present a physical as well as a visual problem. You can counteract this up to a point by using trees or walls to give vertical emphasis and balance but a better solution would be to create level platforms of ground at intervals. These could become separate garden 'rooms' in their own right, each having a different theme or purpose. Whichever you do, keep in mind the point made in Chapter 2: if you progress from an 'architectural' style close to your house, e.g. brick walls close to a brick house, to informality at a distance, e.g. planted or grass banks, you will create a feeling of space. The original slope might be allowed to return at the top or bottom of your garden where it links with the natural countryside or fades into the planting of a more urban setting.

c The creation of steep linking banks or walls affects the amount of light or shade in the immediate vicinity. This means that where planting might have been in a relatively open situation, albeit a north-facing one, it could now be plunged into deep shade by the wall or bank immediately behind it. This will obviously influence the subsequent choice of plant material.

d Retaining walls and steps focus attention and in the case of steps draw both feet and eye to a 'tension point' in the overall design. The design and construction of steps are covered in Chapter 5, 'Hard landscape'.

Where can I see the effects of using different levels?

You can learn a great deal about the use of different levels from the parks and gardens surrounding English historic houses.

In historical terms the great English landscape school of Kent, Brown and Repton (see 'Further reading') fully appreciated the subtleties of a gently rolling scene that flowed from higher to lower ground and from woodland to lake. Such contouring usually hid the boundaries of the estate and created a feeling of space and movement that often belied the true areas involved. Tree planting reinforced the composition and in order to integrate the park and countryside or separate cattle, which were part of this scene, from the house, a dry ditch or 'ha-ha' was used (see Figure 3.1). This eliminated the need for a fence, which would have been visually intrusive.

Figure 3.1 By building a dry ditch and wall (a 'ha-ha') the view from inside a park or large garden can flow into the landscape.

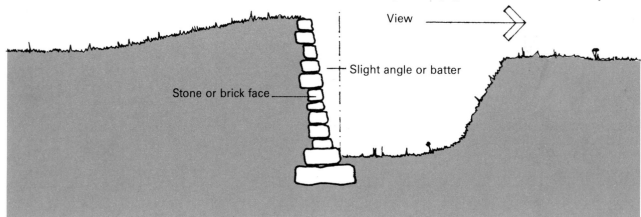

View

Slight angle or batter

Stone or brick face

In many cases the bones of such ground shaping were already present but where they were not they were created on the 'cut-and-fill' principle. Material was excavated to form lakes and used to create higher ground. Incidentally, such hillocks were sometimes hosts for chambers in which ice was stored. This was cut from the lakes in winter for use the following summer. It is amusing to note that the process has come full circle in many a suburban garden where a derelict air-raid shelter, buried under some inconspicuous mound, has become a wine cellar!

In direct contrast to shaping ground in a soft, flowing and natural manner, there are gardens, such as that of Dartington Hall in Devon, where a fourteenth century medieval jousting pit is the basis for a superb series of grass terraces. This stunningly simple and direct approach is the perfect foil for mature trees and largely evergreen plants that make up the rest of the composition.

● Try to carry out one of the following:

a Visit as many large gardens, such as National Trust estates, as you can, and look at the use of different levels.

b Visit your library and find books showing photographs of large gardens. These will give you an idea of how different levels look in practice.

CREATING DIFFERENT LEVELS

From what has been said already in this chapter and from what you have been able to look at for yourself, you can see that there are two methods of approach you can follow when you are creating different levels – the natural approach and the artificial approach.

a You can modify the existing landform in a direct imitation of nature using the undulating slopes and depressions or achieve much the same effect using the 'cut-and-fill' technique. This gives a restful effect and is suitable for both large and small gardens.

b You can create strongly chiselled banks that drop or climb in a series of 'architectural' terraces. These are less restful and are most suitable for large, formal settings, perhaps close to the house.

It is clear, therefore, that the first, softly contoured, approach is the better one to use for a small or average-size garden.

So when you are creating a garden with elements of the natural landscape you must respect what happens in the real world. Very rarely do you see a hill in isolation, a straight valley or a rigidly planted wood (Forestry Commission land excepted). Neither should you see these things in a garden. If you are considering using mounds then make them gently shaped.

In addition to the visual satisfaction of a gentle slope, the practicalities of maintenance also apply. Steep banks are all but impossible to cut except using a hover mower,

while sudden transitions from slopes to horizontal surfaces are equally difficult, preventing the mower from cutting evenly.

It is with these considerations in mind that the benefits of your site plan (see Chapter 2) become evident as you can plot the shape, size and position of contours on this in a practical way.

Contour drawings

● Simple contours can be worked out on a separate copy of the site plan and these can be useful when working out the quantities of soil involved should you need to import this. To superimpose all the contour lines on your design (ground plan) can become complicated and it is usually most simple to indicate the *extent* of any mounds, rather than every detail.

The preparation of a contour drawing is very straight-forward and is undertaken in two stages.

By the use of boning rods (see Chapter 1) you will have ascertained the changes in level involved as well as the steepness of any slope. The purpose of the contour drawing is either to plot these measurements, or to show the height and extent of a new mound.

Lay a copy of the site plan on tracing paper over the grid on which it was prepared. Use the same scale of, say, one square representing 1 m. As you are indicating vertical distances as well as the shape of contours you will need to draw a series of lines, one inside the other, that join all places of the same height. This is clearly shown in Figure 3.2. In this case the contours are indicated at intervals of 25 cm, up to a maximum of 75 cm.

Mounds should appear to be of a similar size. Bear in mind that in elevation, as opposed to plan, distance reduces apparent size, so a large hillock some way away could appear to have similar dimensions to a smaller mound close to the viewer.

Because slopes should be gentle – a slope of 35° is usually an absolute maximum – the higher the mound, the larger the overall contoured area will be. In the average garden situation this means that heights will not be great – and they do not need to be – but a certain amount of space can be saved if the back of the mound is unobtrusively retained by a wall, as in Figure 3.2. Retaining walls are discussed in more detail in Chapter 4.

Many people find it difficult to visualise changes of level, but once you have plotted your contours on your plan you can transfer them to a sectional drawing (refer back to Figure 3.2). The contour lines in plan form indicate the *outline* of the raised areas. If you want to see what a section through any given point looks like, follow this procedure:

● On a piece of tracing paper trace off the contour lines from the contour plan already prepared. Exactly below the plan, on the same piece of paper, indicate the position of the retaining wall. Draw lines across the page to show the vertical heights involved, spacing them using a similar scale to that used on the contour plan. A line AB is drawn across the contour plan where you wish to take a section. Where this line crosses the previously indicated contour lines, extend lines downwards to meet the appropriate horizontal lines on the sectional drawing. In other words, two lines drop down from the 75 cm contour, one line from the 50 cm contour and so on. When these lines are joined together on the sectional drawing, the line of the slope can be indicated (see Figure 3.2).

Your sectional drawing not only gives you an accurate picture of the finished article but makes estimating any quantities of soil needed a simple operation.

By looking at contour plans and sections you will see that within contour lines there is a column of soil that reaches down to the ground. In other words, within the 75 cm contour line that measures, say, 100 cm by 130 cm on the contour plan, this column is 75 cm high. To work out the volume, multiply 100 cm by 130 cm to find the area (1.3 m²) and multiply this by the depth (75 cm) = 0.75 × 1.3 = 0.975 m³. Repeat this operation for the ground within each contour line and add the totals together.

When you undertake any kind of excavation in your garden be sure to separate the subsoil and topsoil, the latter being the fertile, more friable material close to the surface. The depth of topsoil will vary depending on the local conditions. Bear in mind that such soil is organically 'alive' and tends to deteriorate if stacked in large heaps for periods exceeding three months.

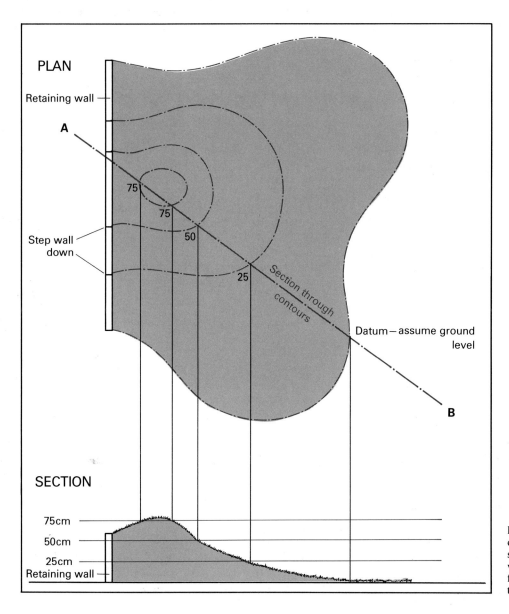

Figure 3.2 By drawing contours in plan (top) and section (beneath) you can visualise finished slopes. The further apart the contour lines, the gentler the gradient will be.

Changing levels around existing trees and other plants

By changing levels you will alter the height of the water-table in different parts of the garden, and this in turn will affect any existing plant material, be it trees or smaller shrubs. Trees in particular are susceptible to changes in soil level around their root systems as this can alter the available oxygen that can be taken up. If ground needs to be built up in the vicinity of a mature tree a well must be left around the bole at least 60 cm from the trunk. Do this by building a wall around the tree to a similar height as the finished ground level and subsequently backfill around the outside. The well itself must be kept clear of rubbish and if the ground is heavy a radiating pattern of drains should be laid to remove water. Where the roots are only partially covered you can sweep a retaining wall around the tree, and allow horizontal drains to exit through the face of the wall. Additional aeration of the root system can sometimes be beneficial for hardwood trees such as beech and oak and in this case vertical tile drains should run down from the surface to connect with the horizontal ring pattern that surrounds the tree (see Figure 3.3).

If the general level is to be lowered, rather than raised, again the roots must be protected and you can do this by leaving a platform around the tree which can be retained by walls or banking. The extent of a root system corresponds roughly with the spread of the canopy and a platform of that size will be the minimum required. Remember, too, that it is the capillary roots at the extremities of the system that gather nourishment and it is these in particular that need protection.

Smaller plants such as hardy perennials, shrubs and young trees can usually be moved safely during their dormant season. Make sure that they are replanted as soon as possible in a suitably prepared hole and are not only well staked and tied but also watered.

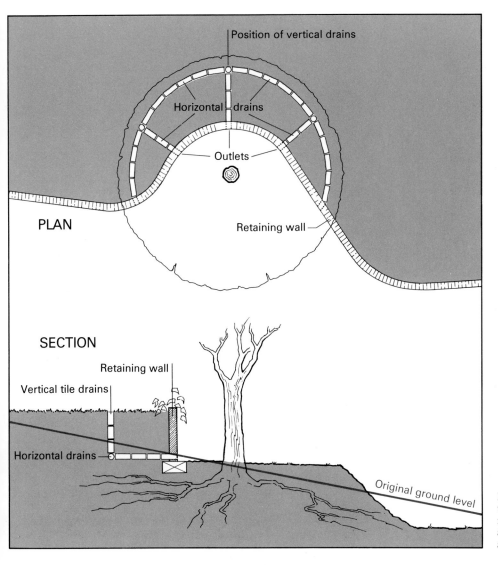

Figure 3.3 Care must be taken to minimise disturbance around mature trees. Good drainage around the roots, coupled with aeration, is essential.

Contouring the garden

The question of whether you carry out the contouring yourself or employ a contractor really comes down to a matter of the scale of the job. Capability Brown used men and wheelbarrows to build hills of considerable size and, of course, you could do the same; but it would take time. If you feel that you have time to tackle the job, then do so. If you feel this is not the case, then employ someone to do it for you. Common sense will quite simply dictate what you can or cannot tackle.

Any work that a contractor does must be supervised closely to make sure that you get the gently modelled composition you have planned and not something that resembles a quarry!

If you contour your garden yourself you will need the following equipment: spade, shovel, pickaxe, wheelbarrow, and scaffold boards (to act as runways for wheelbarrows).

● Once you have collected together your equipment you are ready to start work.

a Peg out the shape of the contours you have worked out on your scale drawing. Do this by scaling off the appropriate measurements with a ruler. For example, 2.5 cm on the drawing may represent 120 cm on the ground. Bamboo canes can be used to mark the extent of the contours and in order to visualise the finished shape you can join them together with string.

b Contours can be built up a layer at a time, topsoil being barrowed in over carefully positioned boards and spread with a shovel. Thoroughly tread over the surface to consolidate each layer before you add the next. Check the shape of the developing mound on the contour plan and sectional drawing. Once the mound is complete, rake it off to make any final adjustments. This is very much a job to be done 'by eye'. The drawing is only a guide and cannot dictate what 'looks' and 'feels' right.

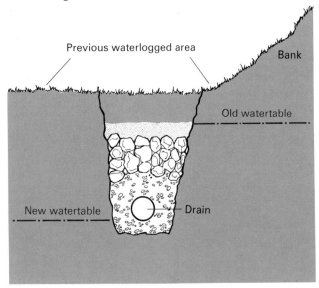

DRAINAGE

The drainage pattern of your garden may well have been altered by the changes you've made in levels, and you may now find that any area that has been compacted or has non-porous soil is susceptible to waterlogging. Indications of this are not only standing water but the failure of plants to grow properly; they may even die altogether. This is because plants gather both water and oxygen from the upper layers of the soil; waterlogging excludes oxygen with harmful consequences.

Moss is often an indicator of poor drainage on lawn areas, but if the problem is not too severe simple spiking with a garden fork or other more specialised tool will provide adequate aeration. Heavy clay soils are the most water-retentive but, contrary to the wealth of confusing advice written on the subject, drainage in everyday gardening terms is quite simple.

Soak-aways

In many situations water gathers in a particular spot, leaving the rest of the garden in a reasonable condition. All that is necessary here is to make a soak-away.

● Remove any topsoil for re-use and then dig a hole 120–180 cm deep and 90 cm square. Fill the hole with clean rubble, hardcore or crushed stone and top this with a 15 cm layer of ash, which prevents soil from clogging the coarser material below. Replace or backfill with topsoil and, if in a lawn area, turf over the disturbed ground.

Drains

In some cases – and this often occurs on sloping sites – water runs on to the garden from higher land. Here you can lay a French or tile drain around the foot of the bank, to direct the water into a suitable ditch or soak-away at a lower level (see Figure 3.4).

French drains are simply ditches filled with clean hardcore, topped with ash or brushwood and finally covered with soil. While this is a cheap and quick method of solving a drainage problem, it is relatively short-lived because the top layers quickly become clogged.

Tile drains form the best and most comprehensive drainage system and may be laid either in straight lines or, more commonly, in a herringbone pattern. The depth at which you lay the drains and the distance at which you space the laterals in a herringbone pattern will be influenced by the type of soil you have (see Table 3.1).

The drains should run at a shallow gradient of approximately 1 in 200 and the outfall should preferably be into a ditch or, failing that, a large soak-away (see Figure 3.5) Use clay pipes. Bed these on an 8 cm layer of gravel in trenches that are approximately 60 cm deep on a heavy soil. Place broken crocks over the joints between the pipes and place a 23 cm layer of gravel on top of these. Fill

Figure 3.4 By inserting a drain at the bottom of a bank you can effectively lower the watertable and eliminate a previously wet area.

Soil type	Spacing of drains (m)	Approximate depth (cm)
CLAY	4.55	60
SAND	9.15	105
LOAM	8.20	90

Table 3.1 **Spacing and depth of tile drains**

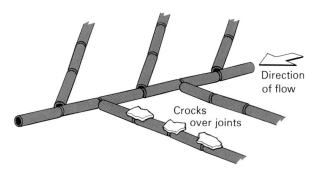

Figure 3.5 Herringbone drain (top) shown (below) discharging into a soak-away.

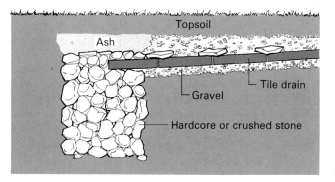

the remaining trench with clean topsoil. (For further details see *The Lawn* by George R. Shiels, also in this series.)

Drainage problems are indicative of soil condition and the rule of treating the cause, not the symptom, is applicable here. The sensible addition of leaf-mould, ash, sand, peat, manure with plenty of straw and well-rotted compost will help to produce a more friable and open soil.

CHECKPOINT

Now that you have finished this chapter you should have decided what kind of contouring is most suitable for your garden, plotted contours on a scale plan and transferred these to a sectional drawing so that you can see what the final effect will be. You should also be able to protect mature trees from the impact of changes in levels and to introduce appropriate forms of drainage into your garden if necessary.

To check that you have fully understood the points covered in this chapter, answer the following questions.

1 What is the effect of a slope going *up* from a house?
2 In what two ways could you counteract the feeling of instability from ground sloping away from your house?
3 What is the 'cut-and-fill' technique?
4 If you are using mounds in your garden what is the maximum degree of slope you should aim for?
5 What is the practical advantage of creating only gentle slopes in your garden?
6 For what kind of drainage problem would you use a soak-away and how would you construct it?
7 At what depth would you lay a tile drain in a heavy clay soil and how far apart would you space the laterals?
8 If you wanted to introduce a gentle mound into your garden but you needed to save space what would you do?
9 How can you estimate how much soil you are likely to need to contour your garden?
10 Give one advantage and one disadvantage of using a French drain.

Check your answers against the information given in the chapter.

CHAPTER FOUR

Walls and fences

Although you probably think of a garden as a complete composition, it is in fact a subtle blend of a great number of separate components and these need to be contained within some sort of boundary. In previous chapters I have discussed the design of your garden and you are probably well on the way to deciding what type of wall or fence you need around it. Alternatively, you may have decided that neither is appropriate in an open-plan or rural setting. In that case you can use this chapter to help you choose any internal screens you may need. Walls and fences play a vital role in dividing garden space as well as being used for screening and shelter. Hedges serve the same purpose and are discussed in Chapter 7, 'Plants and planting design'.

What does a boundary do?

In basic terms a boundary can do several things. It can:

a enclose an area, providing security by preventing people or animals from getting in and out;

b give shelter from the elements, noise and pollution;

c act as a visual barrier, screening unwanted views and stopping people looking in;

d act as a frame, blocking part of the view and emphasising another aspect.

How do I choose the right material?

As with other elements of the garden there is a wide choice of materials available from which to make a boundary and you only have to look at any suburban scene to see just how badly mixed up they can become. Keep in mind the basic rule of compatibility that I mentioned earlier: the style of your house, together with local building practices, should influence your choice. For example, brick or stone walls adjoining houses of similar construction obviously provide an excellent link between inside and out, while the use of traditional fencing, such as wattle hurdles or osiers, still looks good in certain parts of the country. Cost is, of course, a vital factor and if you find walling too expensive, fencing will probably be your second choice, but again try to relate it to the style or colour used in the adjoining building. Ranch fencing, for instance, has been greatly over-used in recent years on new housing estates, but it looks good if it continues a particular architectural line of the building or echoes a colour scheme used on woodwork close by.

It is also worth bearing in mind that you have a certain moral obligation when constructing your boundary. Other local residents will have to live with it, too. A view from the street, largely unsoftened by planting, will become a major element in the town- or village-scape. Although open-plan front gardens have their drawbacks, they can also provide a very restful setting for a street or development.

Table 4.1 compares the advantages and disadvantages of walls and fences and should be used to help you decide which is right for you. Once you have decided whether you will use a wall or fence for your boundary, you should visit your local garden centre or garden shop and look at the materials on offer to see which might be suitable for you.

The next three sections of this chapter will consider walls – what they can be made from and how to build them – and at different types of fencing.

Table 4.1 **Comparison of the advantages and disadvantages of walls and fences**

	Advantage	Disadvantage
Walls	Durable Reduce noise Offer shelter Offer privacy	Expensive, therefore often limited to short runs Difficult to erect
Fences	Cheaper than walls Easier to erect Some types allow a view while providing a barrier	Less durable than walls Less capable of reducing noise Higher maintenance Access needed for maintenance, e.g. path between fence and planted area

FREE-STANDING WALLS

Remember that your choice of material from which to build your wall should link directly to your local setting, but height is also important. If you require privacy a wall of approximately 2 m is a reasonable minimum, but in certain areas, particularly in front gardens or conservation areas, there may well be constraints on both height and material. If in doubt, consult the planning department of your local council.

In certain parts of the country turf or stone-faced banks are common, while the ha-ha mentioned in Chapter 3 is the ultimate link between landscape and garden. Remember that in a rural setting a worthwhile view can be encompassed and your garden is as much out there, in visual terms, as it is within physical boundaries.

To help you choose your walling material brick, stone and concrete will be discussed in turn.

Brick

Brick is the most widely available walling material and comes in a vast range of finishes. Assuming that you have chosen the colour, the next most important factor to con-sider is durability because a free-standing wall is exposed to weathering on both faces. In visual and structural terms a 23 cm wall (two bricks thick) is the most satisfactory. For heights of up to 2 m buttresses that support the wall are not normally necessary and the walls can be finished neatly at the top with a brick-on-edge coping (bricks laid side-by-side), although this could be either stone or a neat, but solid, pre-cast concrete strip, depending on what materials are available (see Figures 4.1 and 4.2).

Brick walls of 11.5 cm thickness, although cheaper, are less strong and look flimsy, particularly when they adjoin a building. They need buttresses at frequent intervals and coping is always a problem. The solution of standing bricks on end, or at an angle, simply aggravates the visual problem. A curved wall is always stronger than a straight run, while if a wall is staggered (Figure 4.3), with one section set behind another, the need for buttressing can often be eliminated. It is worth bearing in mind that by using a curve or a stagger you will create differences in shadow and the angle of lighting, which could be an important consideration when you plan a long run.

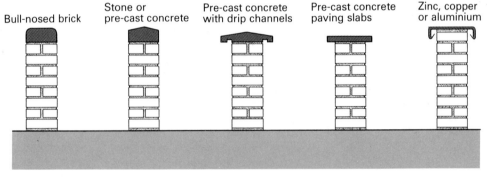

Bull-nosed brick   Stone or pre-cast concrete   Pre-cast concrete with drip channels   Pre-cast concrete paving slabs   Zinc, copper or aluminium

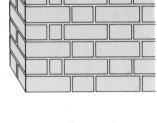

Figure 4.1 Coping seals the top of a wall, preventing the penetration of moisture. Any coping should respect the style used locally and can be brick, stone, concrete or metal.

Figure 4.2 Brick-on-edge is perhaps one of the most unobtrusive and sensible copings available, being used in conjunction with brick or concrete block walls.

Figure 4.3 A single brick wall can be given added strength if the wall is staggered. This pattern could be reinforced by planting and climbers to build up an interesting composition.

A variation on the 11.5 cm brick wall is a honeycomb or pierced wall (see Figure 4.4). In this case the bricks are laid with a joint 7.5–10.0 cm wide. Such walls can form attractive divisions within the garden as they allow a partial view through them. They also, in many situations, look far better than the ubiquitous concrete screen block, often providing a far better link between house and garden. Privacy is obviously limited but you can use them as a wind-break because the gaps slow the wind and reduce turbulence.

There are various points to consider before you begin to build your wall.

Foundations or footings, are the base on which walls stand (see Figure 4.5). They should be constructed from concrete and always be at least twice as wide as the wall itself. The depth of foundation will depend on the height of wall and the type of soil, but for garden purposes a minimum of about 23 cm is preferable.

A damp proof course (Figure 4.6) prevents moisture penetrating up the wall and therefore minimises frost damage. Traditionally, two or three courses (or layers) of a hard 'engineering' brick, slate or even lead were used, the first of these often having a decorative quality as the colour was different from the bricks used in the main part of the wall. Today a bituminous strip is both easy to lay and cheap to buy and if you build a wall from scratch is well worth incorporating.

Expansion joints. Owing to fluctuations in temperature, ground movement and, in this day and age, traffic vibration, a wall is likely to move slightly along its length. Runs of less than about 10 m are unlikely to be affected but if longer a 1.5 cm gap should be incorporated every 8 to 10 m. This is particularly important where a wall meets a house as an ugly crack does nothing to enhance beauty or the goodwill of a building society surveyor.

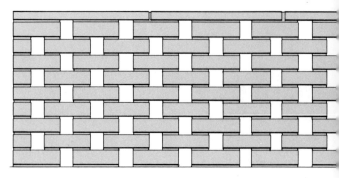

Figure 4.4 A honeycomb brick wall uses wide joints to provide a screen rather than a solid division. It is often more successful than a concrete screen block wall and can be used within the garden to separate different areas. It is also a useful wind-break, forming a semi-permeable screen.

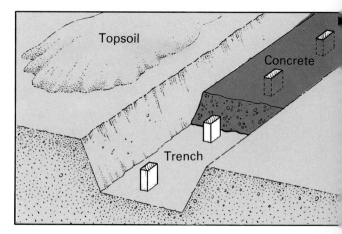

Figure 4.5 Foundations are essential under a wall and if the ground is soft a solid base of hardcore will be needed. Drive level pegs into the sub-base to ensure that the top of the foundation is level and keep this slightly below the finished ground level so that it will not be visible once the wall is built.

Figure 4.7 Brick wall bonds (below).

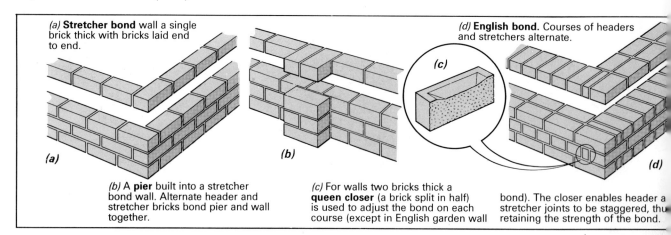

(a) **Stretcher bond** wall a single brick thick with bricks laid end to end.

(b) A **pier** built into a stretcher bond wall. Alternate header and stretcher bricks bond pier and wall together.

(c) For walls two bricks thick a **queen closer** (a brick split in half) is used to adjust the bond on each course (except in English garden wall

(d) **English bond.** Courses of headers and stretchers alternate.

bond). The closer enables header and stretcher joints to be staggered, thus retaining the strength of the bond.

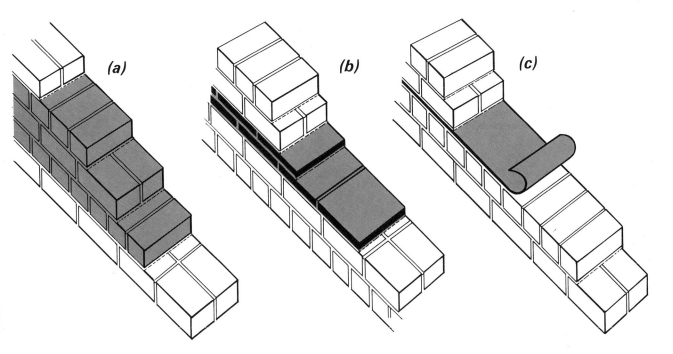

Bonding. Brick bonds are simply the pattern in which bricks are laid to increase the inherent strength of the wall (see Figure 4.7). If joints are aligned, one above the other, then rigidity is lost. In a 23 cm wall bricks are laid both lengthways (stretchers) and through the wall (headers) to bind the whole structure together and to make it, in effect, a homogeneous mass. Not only do bonds have practical value but they are decorative too. Flemish, English, and English garden walling bond are three different patterns.

Pointing is the mortar filling the joints between the bricks. Brick is a modular material and the way in which the joints are finished or 'pointed' has a dramatic effect on the final appearance. Pointing (see Figure 4.8) can be left flush, weathered, keyed, rubbed back or raked out, each of these showing off each module increasingly strongly, light and shadow again playing an important role.

Figure 4.6 Damp proof courses prevent moisture rising up a wall. They can be made from *(a)* three courses of engineering brick, *(b)* two courses of overlapping slates, or *(c)* a roll of bituminous strip. The surrounding ground should be kept two courses below the damp proof course.

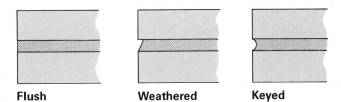

Flush **Weathered** **Keyed**

Figure 4.8 Three types of pointing, flush, weathered and keyed. Each of these produces a different effect. The deeper the joint, the more clearly each module is emphasised.

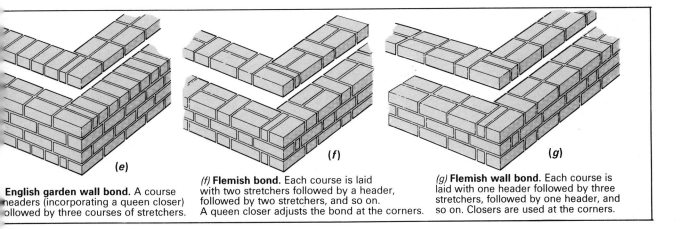

(e) English garden wall bond. A course of headers (incorporating a queen closer) followed by three courses of stretchers.

(f) Flemish bond. Each course is laid with two stretchers followed by a header, followed by two stretchers, and so on. A queen closer adjusts the bond at the corners.

(g) Flemish wall bond. Each course is laid with one header followed by three stretchers, followed by one header, and so on. Closers are used at the corners.

Could I build a brick wall myself?

The question of whether to build the wall yourself or to use a contractor does not relate simply to the amount of time you have available. Laying brickwork is a careful business and you need practice and a degree of skill to produce a worthwhile end result. You will know your own capabilities and you will also know what degree of professionalism you expect in the finished product.

If you decide to undertake the work yourself you will need 50 bricks per square metre of an 11.5 cm wall and 100 bricks per square metre of a 23 cm wall. A mortar mix of four parts sand and one part cement, with the addition of a plasticiser, will be ideal.

Stone

The great difference between brick and stone, apart from aesthetic considerations, is the inequality in size between one piece of stone and another. Where brick is uniform, stone is not and has inevitably a more rural character. True, stone can be cut precisely into blocks as seen in such superb settings as Bath or Cheltenham, but those are not really domestic garden situations.

Could I build a stone wall myself?

Because of its random sizing, stone is not easy to lay and unless you are a craftsman this is a job best left to the professionals. Traditionally mortar was seldom used and the modern preference for wide joints with mortar squashing out like toothpaste does nothing but degrade the material.

Walls can be laid either in courses like bricks or blocks but with larger stones occupying 5.0 cm or 7.5 cm vertical courses or in a completely random pattern where stones of different sizes are fitted together in much the same way as a jigsaw puzzle. Sometimes materials are mixed, for example panels of flint framed by brick.

The foundations of stone walls used to consist of large flat stones but these have been replaced largely by concrete. Again, because of the nature and unevenness of the material, stone walls are usually built to a 'batter', that is, the bottom of the wall is slightly wider than the top. For all practical purposes about 2 m is a sensible maximum height.

The wide joints in a stone wall are perfect places for plants to grow – sometimes self-seeded but often planted – and these look most attractive. You can encourage all but the most rampant plants as their roots will do minimal damage. The practice of ripping vegetation from walls in the fear that they will collapse is encouraged by insensitive architects and over-zealous surveyors. It has no foundation in fact and need not be carried out.

Concrete blocks

Concrete is a much-maligned material and a smooth-faced block makes not only an eminently sensible wall, particularly in a contemporary setting, but also a wall that is far quicker to build than one of stone or brick. Blocks normally measure about $22.5 \times 22.5 \times 45.0$ cm and you can either render or, if well-laid, colour-wash them. A brick-on-edge coping is probably the most satisfactory way to finish the top of the wall. Bold-leaved climbers look particularly handsome against such a simple background.

Concrete screen blocks come in an alarming number of patterns, many of which are far too complicated. They do not provide privacy nor do they prevent draughts. In all but the simplest patterns they 'tart up' a garden and it is well worth thinking about using a honeycomb brick wall or some other material. If you do use them, soften the outline with copious planting and rampant climbers. In the end the wall becomes incidental.

There are a number of far simpler and better-designed blocks now on the market. The 'landscape bloc' (Figure 4.9) is available in a wide range of sizes and can be laid in a number of patterns that set up endless permutations.

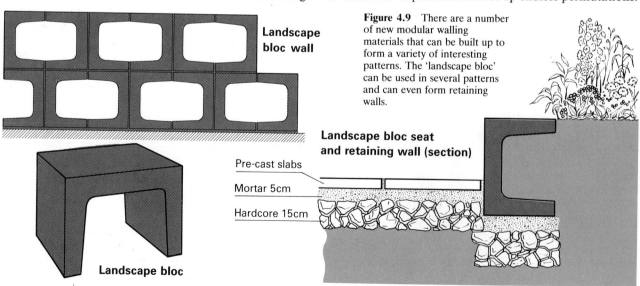

Landscape bloc wall

Figure 4.9 There are a number of new modular walling materials that can be built up to form a variety of interesting patterns. The 'landscape bloc' can be used in several patterns and can even form retaining walls.

Landscape bloc seat and retaining wall (section)

Pre-cast slabs
Mortar 5cm
Hardcore 15cm

Landscape bloc

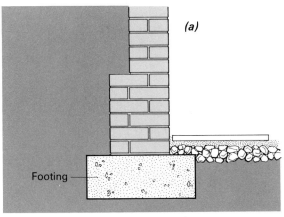

Figure 4.10 Retaining walls.

(a) A brick retaining wall can be built thicker at the bottom to provide greater stability. Always ensure that there is an adequate foundation.

(b) Mass cast concrete can provide a useful retaining wall in an architectural situation, or it can alternatively be faced with brick or stone. One of the advantages of concrete is that a 'toe' can be cast, giving stability and helping to prevent the wall being pushed over by soil pressure.

(c) A raised bed is simply a series of retaining walls. Hardcore or other free-draining material can be placed at the bottom of the bed, joints in brickwork being left open as 'weep holes'.

(d) A cavity wall can prevent water staining the facework of a wall. Concrete blocks, brick or cast concrete could be used for the inner face.

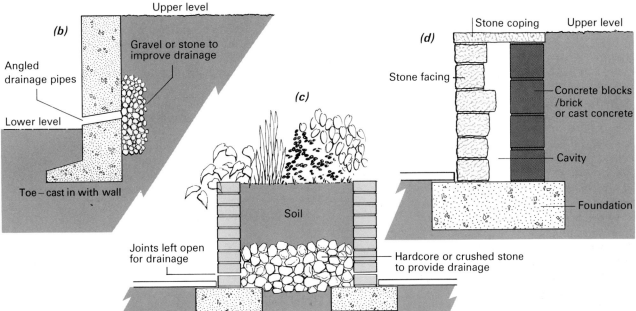

This sort of design is entirely laudable and brings a breath of fresh air to an otherwise tired subject.

RETAINING WALLS

Free-standing walls are just what their name suggests they are. Retaining walls (Figure 4.10) hold back a bank at a higher level and often form the division between the terraces in a sloping garden.

Where such a wall is called for, the broad aesthetic principle regarding the choice of material, which has already been mentioned, should be adhered to. The major problem is the action and pressure of water at the back of the wall. If the wall needs to be more than 1.2 m high, this is a job best left to a contractor, who should enlist the services of a structural engineer to prepare a full specification.

Greatest pressure on a wall is caused by loose, light soil and is most apparent at the base. In basic terms the wall should be thickest at the bottom. If a wall is built in brick it can be two courses (46 cm) wide for the first six courses, this width being positioned on the inside of the wall, reducing to one course (23 cm) above this.

A mass concrete wall can be cast so that the bottom is thicker than the top and it can also incorporate a 'toe' that digs into the ground under pressure to provide greater stability.

Water in the ground increases presssure and this should be relieved by drainage or 'weep' holes every 1.2 m along the bottom of the wall, 7.5 cm above the ground. Such holes can take the form of pipes set at a slight angle, neatly cut off flush with the face, or you can leave open joints at similar intervals in brick or stone walls. In order to improve drainage through the holes, lay a strip of gravel or crushed stone behind them, 30 cm wide and the same deep. This should be positioned over a sheet of polythene or concrete which will reduce the amount of water working its way under the wall which might cause the whole structure to slide forward.

FENCES (see Figure 4.11)

All fences need to be given a regular coat of non-toxic preservative. Never use creosote because it is highly toxic to plants. Depending on the type of construction, the life expectancy will vary and the traditional wattle hurdles will, for instance, decay in between six and eight years. Such a fence is relatively cheap to buy and forms the ideal shelter for a young hedge, which can be well on the way to maturity by the time the fence is finally removed. As with walling, respect any local styles of fencing – which may well be cheaper to buy – and remember that the much-loved suburban rustic fence or screen, which comes complete with bark, not only looks incongruous but quickly rots. Always remove bark from timber as it simply traps moisture and accelerates decay.

Remember, too, that honesty is another design rule. The plastic post-and-chain fence and the pretentious way in which it is used detracts from the charm that this type of boundary has in the correct setting. Similarly, plastic ranch fencing sets out to ape the real thing and as a result looks phoney.

Sensible construction that includes capping of panels and posts, regular maintenance and the use of gravel boards at the bottom will all pay dividends in the long run. Gravel boards are fitted along the bottom of a fence, retaining the surrounding soil and thus protecting the fence panels. If they rot they can be replaced relatively easily and cheaply. Where possible – and this applies to virtually all fence types – try to use hardwood posts that have a far longer lifespan than softwood. It is the post that takes all the strain, so spend a little more initially. Posts should always be kept flush with the top of any fence and the normal practice of letting them protrude by several inches has an unsettling influence on the run as a whole. In legal terms the posts and arris rails (to which boards are nailed) are normally set on the side of boundary ownership.

The types of fencing from which you can choose are set out below. As you make your choice remember that some types of fencing are closed while others are open to allow a view: for example in a rural setting, post-and-rail is stock-proof but allows landscape and garden to run together; in a more urban setting, ranch fencing does much the same thing, but in a far more architectural and controlled manner. Your choice of either closed or open fencing depends on your particular setting.

Closed fencing

Interwoven panels. This is the most popular fence available. It can be purchased in a variety of heights and is reasonably priced. It benefits from being softened by planting and climbers can be trained on wires stretched between the posts; this helps to minimise the contact of moist leaves on the relatively thin slats and so helps to prevent rotting of the wood. Normally the panels are set vertically but think whether this will fit in visually with

Figure 4.11 Fences.

Interwoven

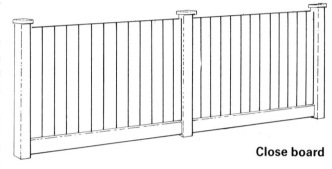

Close board

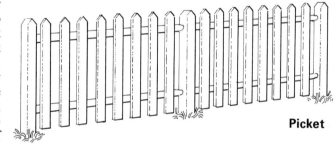

Picket

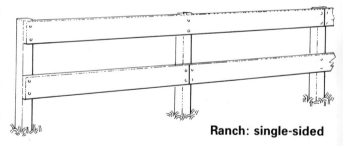

Ranch: single-sided

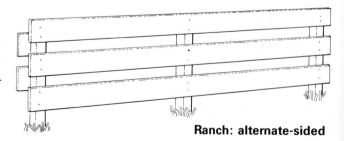

Ranch: alternate-sided

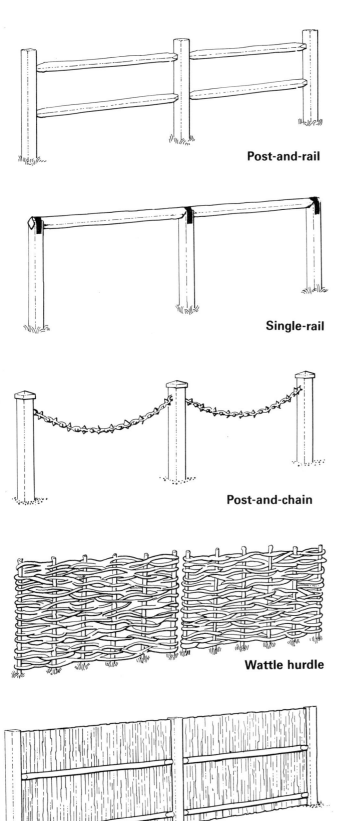

Post-and-rail

Single-rail

Post-and-chain

Wattle hurdle

Norfolk reed

your garden before you automatically follow suit.

Close board. This is a durable but fairly expensive type of fence as posts and arris rails have to be erected and then the boards nailed on to these so that they overlap each other. The direction in which the run of boards is set will have a horizontal emphasis and this could be an important element in your overall garden design, visually helping to widen a space.

Slatted fences. Instead of the boards overlapping each other as mentioned above, they can be spaced with a slight gap in between. This produces a particularly handsome and, again, architectural effect. The boards should normally all be of one width within a run and, if supported on the back, present a clean face to the garden. A smaller version of this is the picket fence which can be attractive in a front garden, painted white. The tops can be either rounded or pointed.

Ranch fencing. This can consist of two or three rails, quite widely spaced, or a solid fence where the rails are fixed on alternate sides of the post, completely breaking the view. In the majority of cases this is made of softwood and therefore needs regular maintenance with paint or preservative. The alternative fixing, which can be horizontal or vertical, produces a striking contrast of light and shadow. Such a fence relates well to modern buildings, helping to continue their clean line out into the garden.

Open fencing

Post-and-rail. While post-and-rail allows a view and prevents the intrusion of stock in a rural situation, it lacks privacy and does nothing to provide shelter. Two- or three-rail versions are normally constructed and this type of fence largely replaced the traditional iron park railings which can still be seen on some estates. The delicacy of iron made it practically invisible at a distance, while the addition of beautiful but simply detailed kissing gates were a lesson in controlled design. Where access is needed through a post-and-rail fence, a stile is perhaps most suitable.

Single-rail. Single-rail fences, in hard- or soft-wood, are low and simply serve as a demarcation. They are neat and architectural and can be used to good effect in a front garden open-plan situation, to define boundaries. The rail normally sits at an angle of 45° in a notch cut out of the verticals, being held in position with a galvanised metal strap.

Post-and-chain. This is a traditional and largely urban version of single-rail fencing. White posts are connected by lengths of black chain and this sort of fence is really only suitable for use outside the façade of a fine building. Its use, in plastic, on housing estates does little to enhance gardens.

Wattle hurdles. Of the traditional patterns, wattle hurdles are probably the most widely available. Originally used for penning sheep, they are woven with hazel. They have a far less clinical appearance than machine-made fences and, although not long-lasting, provide an excellent screen for developing plants.

Reeds and osiers. Where these materials are available locally they provide excellent fences. Osiers are woven horizontally in the same way as hurdles, while reeds are stood upright, sandwiched between horizontal rails. Although particularly fine in a rural setting with cottage architecture, they adapt surprisingly well to a more sub-urban situation where their unobtrusive background brings stability to a developing garden.

Chestnut palings. These are really a traditional form of chain link fencing, chestnut verticals being spaced at approximately 7.5 cm intervals on strands of wire. They do not provide privacy or shelter but are certainly dog-proof and difficult for children to climb. They are usually available in heights up to about 135 cm and the bottoms of the palings should be kept clear of the ground to prevent rot setting in.

Chain link. This familiar fence is eminently practical around factories and tennis courts but has an institutional quality. At a distance, however, set in or between a plan-ted area, it can be virtually invisible and is extremely valu-able where security is needed. Plastic-coated posts and fences are available in a range of colours; black, green and brown are the most suitable for landscape work.

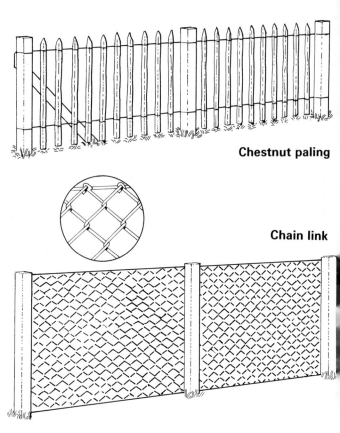

Chestnut paling

Chain link

INTERNAL SCREENS

A partial screen within the garden can often be an import-ant and integral part of the overall composition. While rustic timber is commonly used, it is not particularly handsome and has a limited life. Squared trellis construc-ted from 13 mm or 19 mm timber is a sensible alternative and certainly has a crisper, no-nonsense outline.

Scaffold poles

An attractive screen can be built from scaffold poles, set in concrete (see Figure 4.12). Plug the tops with timber dowels, space the holes about 15 cm apart, and then paint it and run climbers over the structure. Incidentally, the paler you paint a screen, the more light it reflects and the more difficult it is to see through: white screens block the view while black screens allow it to run through.

Fedge

While a hedge is purely vegetative, a fedge is a hybrid between a fence and a hedge. It usually consists of a wire framework, which can be bent to any shape and forms a basis for a planting of rampant climbers. These quickly soften the entire structure and varieties of honeysuckle, ivy or clematis will provide a display that gives colour and interest through the year.

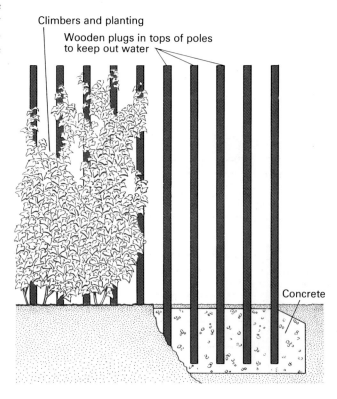

Climbers and planting

Wooden plugs in tops of poles to keep out water

Concrete

Figure 4.12 Scaffold-pole screen.

GATES (see Figure 4.13)

Now that you have considered how to surround your garden and divide it internally, access through it is vital and here the choice of an unsuitable gate can ruin an otherwise sensible composition. Gates should not necessarily match the material used in the boundary; they are quite simply different and need to mark clearly a way in. Simplicity, however, is usually paramount. The visual damage caused by a poorly detailed, so-called wrought iron gate against the clean lines of any kind of wall is enormous. On the other hand a wooden gate that matches the height of a boundary will look fine. Remember, too, that a non-solid gate offers a clear view and there is little point in trying to maintain privacy or shelter if you use one. Conversely, the incongruity of gates, both for people and cars, should be obvious in an open-plan situation. So often you see two gates in a small front garden where the boundary is otherwise minimal. A far better solution would be to define the separate areas by paving and plant-

ing, the latter being rather better at discouraging casual callers than poorly detailed low walls. This will also rationalise any footpath to the front door by integrating it with the drive. Meanness is the enemy of good garden design and far too many front approaches show it.

CHECKPOINT

Now that you have read this chapter you should have decided whether you will use a wall or fence for your boundary and what kind of material is most suitable in your situation. You should also have established what kinds of internal screen, if any, are necessary for your garden and what kind of gate you need. To check that you have understood the points made in this chapter, answer the following questions.

1 What is the basic rule that governs your choice of material for a boundary?
2 What is the most satisfactory thickness for a free-standing wall?
3 For a wall of a certain length, height and thickness, how would you calculate the number of bricks you would need?
4 In what ratio of sand to cement should you mix the mortar for a brick wall?
5 Why is a stone wall more difficult to build than a brick one?
6 If you wanted to build a wall around the garden of your new town house and hadn't much time to spare or experience at building, what material would you use?
7 Give two advantages of using a fence rather than a wall as a boundary.
8 What is a fedge and what would you use one for?
9 List the four main functions of a boundary.
10 Why is it necessary to incorporate a bituminous strip in the building of a brick wall and at what stage in the wall's construction should you include it?

Check your answers against the information given in the chapter.

Figure 4.13 Gates should respect the boundaries in which they are set and the local environment.
(a) A five-bar, diamond-braced gate has an inherently rural flavour.
(b) An iron gate forms an effective but simple foil to massive stone piers.
(c) In an architectural situation a sensibly detailed wrought iron gate can look superb, but avoid cheap suburban imitations!
(d) A combined pedestrian and vehicle gate often simplifies a front boundary. Timber and brick is a particularly good combination.

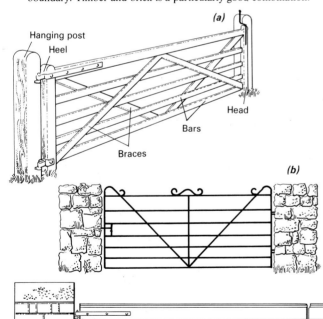

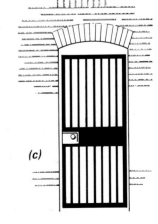

Choosing materials/Man-made materials/Natural materials
Other features of hard landscape
Checkpoint

Once you have decided what kind of wall or fence you will put around your garden and what, if any, internal screens you will have, you can begin to 'fill in' your garden design with paved and planted areas, or, as they can be called in broader terms, hard and soft landscape. I will discuss hard landscape and materials in this chapter and then look at soft landscape in Chapter 6.

How important is the 'hard landscape' in my garden design?

The hard landscape is a key factor in your design for the following reasons:

a It forms the bones of the design, e.g. terrace areas for sitting and dining, paths, drives and hardstanding, and will probably set the theme for the planted areas, lawn and overall proportions of your whole garden.

b As your 'floor', it is the background for a host of activities that will take place on it and therefore must be designed to take these into account.

c It gives that vital first impression: the terrace is usually the first point of access in a garden while at the front of your house you have the paved areas leading to your door.

Have I allowed enough space for paved areas?

On your scale plan you have roughly allocated space for paved or hard areas. You now need to make sure that you have allowed enough space.

As a general rule a sitting area needs to be a minimum of about 3.75 m square, or the size of a small room. This avoids the situation where a chair tips backwards into planting, followed by a guest with a cup of tea! An area of this size allows for tables, chairs, sun-loungers and the inevitable collection of toys that find their way on to any dry, flat surface.

Paths, particularly where they adjoin a border, need to be about 1 m wide and this will be ample for wheeled toys, barrows and lawn-mowers. If you take your path right around your garden it not only makes a sensible mowing edge, eliminating that dreadful chore of hand-edging, but makes a marvellous toy track. There is nothing more frustrating to a child in full flight on a tricycle than having to stop and turn round. Your nerves may become frayed by a race track but your children will love it. Gardens are for the whole family!

A good hardstanding at least 2 m square outside sheds and greenhouses is useful as this is often a point where you park a wide range of tools and equipment.

● Take another look at the paved areas you have roughed in on your scale plan and make any adjustments necessary using the information above.

Could I lay a hard surface myself?

Paving, as opposed to walling, is very much a job you can do yourself. Materials are readily available from builders' merchants and garden centres and laying techniques are straightforward.

If you are going to lay the hard surfaces in your garden yourself, remember that they will need to be laid properly as they will be used intensively at all times of the year. I will deal with the techniques of laying individual materials later in this chapter but there are a few general points to make. All surfaces should be at least two courses below your house damp proof course and fall away from the building. Such a fall need not be great: 1 in 100 is adequate so long as it is constant. It is normally quite sufficient to allow rainwater to soak away into surrounding planting or the adjoining lawn. Where this is difficult, as in the case of a sunken area, the water will need to be directed into a drain. There is an opportunity here, if you are using a combination of two or three paving types, to build up a pattern, perhaps in a grid, where one surface can be laid to form a drainage channel.

CHOOSING MATERIALS

Garden centres sell such a variety of materials for hard surfaces that it is difficult to know how to choose between them. You will find it easier to decide if you consider what you can afford, the characteristics of the materials and how you can use them, and elements of design.

Cost

Your expenses will come from two directions – the cost of the materials and the cost of laying them if you employ a contractor to do the work.

Natural materials such as stone slabs, cobbles and granite setts are usually more expensive than man-made materials. This is partly because of the transport charges involved in carrying them over long distances and partly because quarrying and cutting involves far more labour than moulding a brick or a concrete slab. However, on the other side of that argument, you undoubtedly get what you pay for and natural materials not only last a lifetime but often give the garden that all-important feeling of maturity.

The size of a particular module bears a direct relationship to the cost of laying. For example, a large area of concrete can be put down in a comparatively short time whereas to hand-set cobbles or brick is a lengthy and careful operation and one which is inevitably more costly.

Hard landscape can take up as much as 80 per cent of your garden design budget and so it is very important to get your plans right first before you buy any materials.

Characteristics and use of materials

Here are some examples of the way in which the characteristics of materials determine their use.

a The larger the paved area, the larger the material that should be used. For instance, a wide expanse of drive might be best surfaced in a sweep of gravel or tarmac that will tend to provide continuity. On a small terrace the whole design could be more intimate using smaller modules in a more intricate pattern while still emphasising simplicity.

b The texture of a surface determines the speed and type of traffic that passes over it. Smooth concrete, whether slabs or cast *in situ* (laid on the spot), provides fast, easy access for feet and wheels alike. Bricks or natural stone slabs are slightly uneven, slowing things down a bit, while granite setts or cobbles are positively uncomfortable to walk over and can be laid as a deterrent.

c The way in which you link your house and garden with compatible materials – brick walls with brick paving, stone floors or walls with stone terracing – has a considerable influence on the finished result. Bear in mind that natural stone slabs and pre-cast concrete slabs are best laid to a rectangular pattern as cutting is difficult. Free-form materials such as concrete, gravel or tarmac, however, can be used in a flowing design that can provide a great feeling of space and movement. The smaller the module, the easier it is to lay to a curve: cobbles, bricks, setts and stable pavers can all be fitted into a curving pattern. However, the tighter the curve, the more the joints open up. In some cases you can take advantage of this: for example, if you lay paving slabs as a curving path you can fill the triangular joints with aromatic plants or small cobbles to give an interesting change of texture (see Figure 5.1).

Elements of design

Remember the following points as you make your choice.

First, as with all aspects of design, simplicity is the rule. Keep to this and it will prevent you from falling into the trap of over-complication, mixing materials and ending up with a hotchpotch that is not only garish but unpleasantly restless.

Second, do not be afraid to use materials out of context. Kerb edges, usually measuring about 1 m long and 30 cm wide, make a marvellous paving module when laid flat, while railway sleepers, timber decking and wood blocks can be superb in the right setting. Design is all about individuality and surprise. Mimicry is the antithesis of originality, so think of unusual materials and techniques: some of them can work very well indeed.

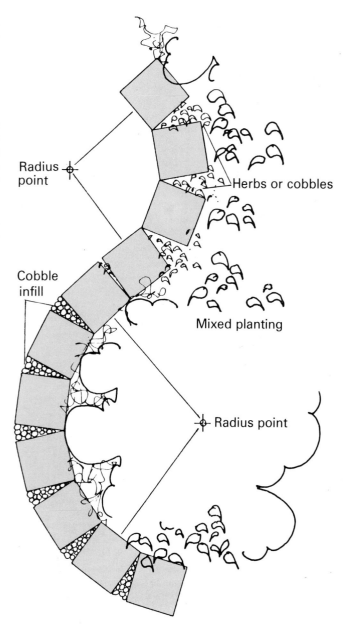

Figure 5.1 Rectangular slabs can be used in a curved path as shown. They are set out to a predetermined radius and the open joints can be either filled with small cobbles or left open for aromatic plants.

MAN-MADE MATERIALS

Concrete slabs and paving blocks

Pre-cast concrete slabs are by far the most popular and widely used paving material. They are reasonably priced and come in a vast range of shapes, colours, sizes and textures. As with most things in the garden, keep the concept simple. Some of the colours available are dreadful and fade to sickly hues. Perhaps the only worthwhile ones are those that honestly try to imitate natural stone and some of these slabs are remarkably good substitutes for the real thing. Since many houses are being built from imitation stone, there is no harm in using a similar slab in a terrace area. This is an honest solution and a good link between inside and out.

When slabs are wet they turn darker and this can completely change the character of an area. Similarly, a dark courtyard can be brought to life by a pale slab that reflects light. Although the common grey paving slabs are just a little coarse for domestic use, some of the other grey slabs on the market are excellent. Remember that grey is a great harmoniser and forms a restful background. To team slabs with bricks or other small modules can work very well, the latter tending to soften the overall surface as well as possibly giving that added link with the house.

Rectangular slabs can be laid either with all the joints coinciding, when the overall effect is static, or with broken joints, where the direction of stagger tends to provide emphasis along that line. This can be useful to open up a narrow space laterally or lead the eye in a particular direction.

Apart from rectangles, there are numerous other shapes available, including hexagonal and circular and most shapes in between. These are often difficult to use in an 'architectural' situation close to the house but can be most effective in more informal parts of a garden. Once again, use the inherent character of the material. It is amazing how often you see hexagonal slabs cut to form a straight path. Not only does this involve a vast amount of labour but it detracts from the basic shape. Hexagons should be allowed to follow a more random pattern that echoes the shape or angles of the module itself (see Figure 5.2). This can look delightful through planting where the two surfaces mingle together.

A fairly recent introduction has been that of concrete paving blocks that can either be rectangular, with the approximate proportions of a brick, or have an interlocking shape (Figure 5.2) so that they fit together rather like a jigsaw. They are immensely strong and, although just a little clinical for a domestic sitting area, can be ideal for a drive or hardstanding. They are also easy to lay, being simply bedded down on a 7.5 cm layer of sharp (concreting) sand over 7.5–10.0 cm of well-consolidated hardcore, and blinded (covered) with sand or ash to remove any irregularities. The blocks should be butted

close together and bedded down with a hired 'plate vibrator'. Sand, brushed into the joints as the vibrator is passed over the surface, finally stabilises the surface. Colours can vary from grey, through a rather insipid pink to an attractive dark brown.

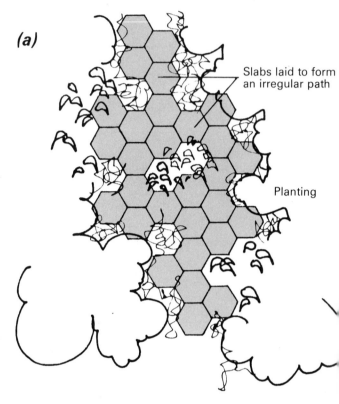

(a)

Slabs laid to form an irregular path

Planting

Figure 5.2   Pre-cast concrete paving can be laid in a variety of patterns and is available in many shapes. Hexagonal paving *(a)* should be laid in a staggered pattern to produce an informal effect. Concrete block pavers *(b)* can be similarly used in an informal path, or used for drives or hardstandings in a more formal setting.

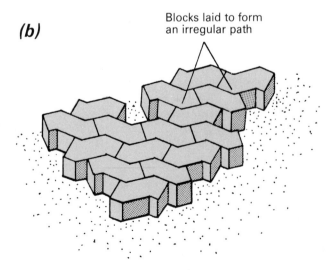

(b)

Blocks laid to form an irregular path

Laying concrete slabs

Concrete slabs are laid slightly differently from paving blocks and there are three basic techniques used. The technique to use depends on the amount of wear a surface is likely to receive.

a For the most simple technique, level the ground and compact it with a heavy roller. Then spread and rake out a layer of sand and bed the slabs on it. Such a surface, although easy to lay, will be subject to subsidence, as the sand can be washed away easily as water works under the edges of the slabs or percolates through the joints.

b You can achieve a more durable result if you first excavate the area and lay a layer of hardcore. This should be about 7.5 cm on firm ground, 15 cm on soft ground, and can be brick or crushed stone. Ram this down well and cover, or 'blind', the surface with a layer of sand or ash, thus filling in any cracks or depressions. You can then position the slabs on five spots of mortar, and tamp them down to reach the correct level. To ensure regular joints between the slabs use wooden spacers, which can be taken out prior to pointing (see Figures 5.3 and 5.4).

c A final method is to lay a foundation as before and then bed the slabs on a continuous layer of mortar (see Figure 5.3). This will be exceptionally durable but the slabs will be hard to lift, a point to be borne in mind should you wish to reach any pipes or services beneath.

Stepping stones through a lawn, or a path around the perimeter, are a positive feature in any design, leading both feet and eye in a required direction. If you use slabs for this purpose they need to be set about 13 mm below the surface of the grass (see Figure 5.3) so that your mower can pass over them without being damaged. To do this, place the slabs in position and mark around the edges with a spade or edging iron. Remove the slab and carefully lift the turf. Excavate to the required depth, making sure the bottom is level, and drop the slab into position.

Pointing

Pointing involves filling the joints between the slabs with mortar. The deeper the joint is 'raked' out, the more emphasis will be placed on each slab, with the resulting shadow line. In some cases, perhaps in an informal area, the joints can be left open, allowing the artificial seeding of low-growing aromatic plants.

In situ concrete

While slabs are cast to a specific shape, concrete can be laid on the spot, or *in situ*, to a wide range of patterns. This could form an architectural composition, possibly in a front garden, squares of concrete being separated by courses of brick, slabs or wood strips. Such dividers have a dual purpose, not only helping to build up the design in visual terms but acting as 'expansion joints'. These are necessary because of the reaction of any large surface to temperature fluctuations and the panels of concrete should be no more than 3 m square, otherwise cracking will soon set in. In a free-form situation you can pour concrete to follow curves, provided a suitable edging is used. The latter could be boards set on edge, a metal strip,

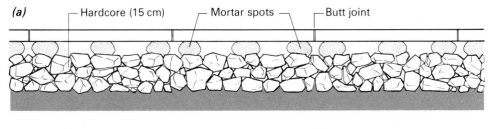

(a) ⌐ Hardcore (15 cm) ⌐ Mortar spots ⌐ Butt joint

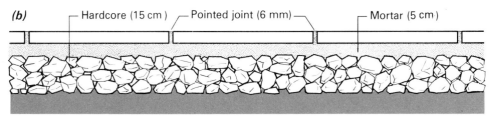

(b) ⌐ Hardcore (15 cm) ⌐ Pointed joint (6 mm) ⌐ Mortar (5 cm)

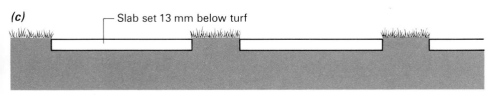

(c) ⌐ Slab set 13 mm below turf

Figure 5.3 Concrete slabs can be laid in three basic ways *(a)* on spots of mortar, *(b)* on a continuous bed of mortar or *(c)* simply on soil or a layer of sand through a lawn area.

bricks or any other similar small module that can be laid to a curve. The use of kerb edges that are usually about 1 m long is not good practice because, although they give the very gentlest curve, they produce a faceted outline which appears restless.

Mixing concrete

A suitable mix for most projects in the garden consists of one part cement, two parts sharp sand and three parts aggregate or small stones, by volume. Always mix the ingredients thoroughly before adding water. Ensure that the mix is wet enough to be worked easily, but do not saturate it, as this weakens the finished concrete.

Figure 5.4 *(a)* Slabs are laid on a prepared base, the area being marked out with strings. *(b)* Spots of mortar are placed to accept the slab and *(c)* the slab is carefully positioned. *(d)* The slab is checked for level using a straight edge and spirit level and *(e)* spacers are inserted as work continues.

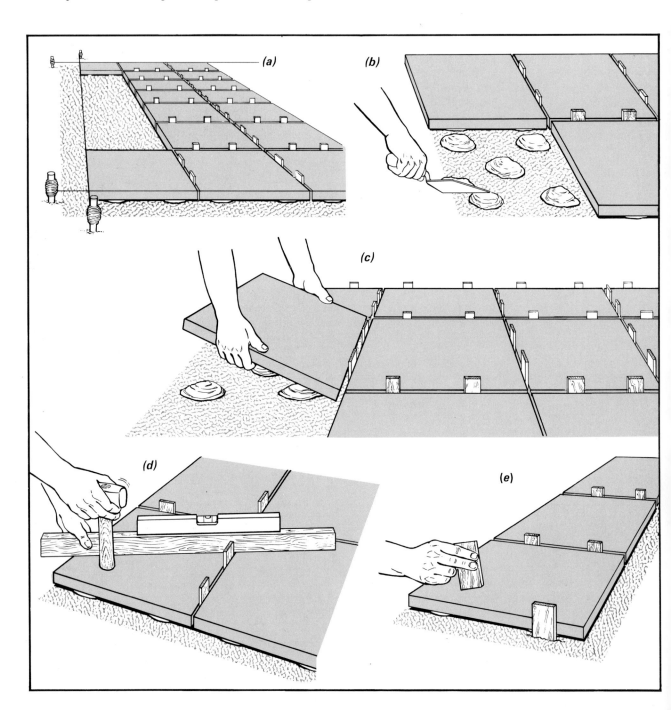

Finishes (see Figure 5.5)

The surface of newly laid concrete can be given different finishes by using different tools: a board tamped across the surface will produce shallow ridges, often useful on a drive; a steel float will polish the surface to a smooth finish; a wooden float will leave a slight texture. Perhaps the most attractive result is achieved by 'brushing'. Do this with a broom just before the concrete goes hard. Carefully water the surface and then brush it to expose the small aggregate stones in the mix. This produces a marbled effect that is full of character.

Always protect concrete that you have laid in either hot or cold conditions. Use dry sacking to protect it from frost, and wet sacks if the temperatures are high. The latter prevents the surface from drying too quickly and is called 'curing'.

NATURAL MATERIALS

Some materials, because of their intimate nature, lend themselves better to small-scale use than to use for large areas of hardstanding or drives.

Stone

This is perhaps the finest, and certainly the most expensive, paving material. Stone can range from locally quarried sandstones to slate and even marble, the latter being somewhat exotic. York stone is widely used and is available in random rectangular sizes or crazy paving. Old York stone is often lifted from cottage and mill floors, but be sure to check the latter as it can be very badly stained with oil. Old York stone also comes in varied thicknesses and a load can have slabs between 5 cm and 10 cm thick, which means you must make considerable adjustments to the foundation levels. New York stone is more expensive, much lighter in colour and of a more uniform thickness. I have already mentioned that care should be taken in laying crazy paving close to a building, but if it is contained within panels of brick or another similar module this does much to stabilise the inherent 'busy' characteristic. However, such paving would be generally far better employed as an informal sitting area, some way from the house. It is also worth bearing in mind that natural stone, in shady areas, tends to pick up algae and become slippery in wet weather.

The weight of slabs allows them to be safely bedded on sand, but make sure that the foundation is porous (i.e. made up of hardcore or open soil), otherwise water will collect and wash the sand away. Because the stone slabs are difficult to cut, the edge of a terrace need not be a straight line – let it die off into lawn or planting in an irregular pattern. Also try to avoid too many joints running together in a straight line. It can be most effective

Figure 5.5 The surface finish of concrete can be varied considerably. Brushing and polishing with various tools produces different end results.

Soft broom finish

Exposed aggregate finish by washing and brushing

Shovel-back finish

Wood float finish

Steel float finish

to start the paving pattern around a central key stone, working the slabs out from this point.

Slate

Slate is an altogether crisper-looking material than stone, rather darker in colour and when wet almost black. It has a beautiful surface texture and a character of its own. Because of its colour it can tone down a surrounding area, but if you team it with paler gravel or white chippings you can set up a most striking contrast.

Marble

Marble is at the other end of the brightness range and needs to be carefully used if it is not to look pretentious. It can look superb for formal steps, perhaps adjoining a house, but this sort of material is really the 'punctuation mark' of hard landscape. It is also extremely expensive.

Cobbles

Cobbles are those marvellous round or oval water-washed stones that you find on the beach or bed of a stream. (It is, incidentally, illegal to take stones from a beach.) You can lay them in formal or informal patterns, coursed or uncoursed. If you set them in concrete you should pack them together as closely as possible, with no background showing. Resist at all costs the dreadful municipal habit of using them like currants in a bun! You can also use them as a pedestrian deterrent because they are uncomfortable to walk on, and they make a most effective 'ground cover', piled loosely among planting with the addition of an occasional larger smooth boulder to provide emphasis.

Another useful application can be in front of a garage, as a panel set within the main paving material. In this situation they will act as an oil drip, effectively disguising stains that would be almost impossible to remove from a smooth surface.

You can lay cobbles in much the same way as slabs, by pressing them into mortar over a layer of sand and hardcore. Tamp the stones down to ensure that the tops are level. An alternative method is to bed them on a dry mortar mix and then carefully water the surface. This prevents mortar from staining the cobbles.

Granite setts

These are solid granite and come in two basic sizes: full setts are roughly the dimensions of a brick; half setts are about half the size. They were originally used for street paving but have since been covered with tarmac. Setts are slightly uneven and therefore not suitable where a perfectly flat surface is necessary. You can, however, use them to great effect on drives and paths where this characteristic will provide grip. They can also be used as a decorative surround at the base of a tree or some other focal point, their small size allowing them to be laid to a tight radius. Many councils are now using them as pavement edges,

but they are not always in keeping with the surrounding buildings. The same problem may apply in a domestic setting. You can lay setts in a similar way to cobbles, with as little mortar as possible showing between the joints.

Brick

Brick is perhaps one of the most versatile paving materials available and has a character completely its own. Because of its size it tends to be used in intimate situations, either by itself or in conjunction with other surfaces, where it has a softening influence. The modern trend of using large areas of brick outside buildings is not always successful and is often boring because the scale of each module is submerged by the overall volume of the material. Brick is time-consuming to lay, as well as being expensive.

Standard bricks measure approximately $23.0 \times 7.5 \times 11.5$ cm while special paving bricks, sometimes called 'slips' or 'paviors', are only about 2.5 cm thick. The range of textures and finishes is legion while the hardness can vary from engineering bricks of exceptional durability to

Stretcher bond
Along path (flat)

Herringbone
Diagonal to path (flat)

Stretcher bond
Across path (on edge)

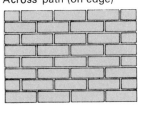

Herringbone
Square to path (on edge)

Soldier courses
Along path (on edge)

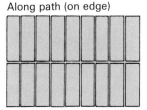

Basketweave (flat)

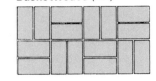

Figure 5.6 Bricks can be laid in three basic patterns, stretcher bond (soldier courses are a variation of this), herringbone and basketweave. In addition to this, bricks can be laid either flat or on edge. With the former technique rather more of the brick surface and less joints are seen. The direction of the bonds provides emphasis in various directions.

soft red 'stocks' which withstand little or no frost. Such inherent characteristics tend to suggest a wide range of applications and while the crisp line of an engineering brick would do much to complement a contemporary building it would be totally out of place beside a half-timbered cottage.

Ideally, the brick used in a scheme adjoining a house should match the house brick, but sometimes the density of the brick makes this impossible. In this case you should try to find a close match but remember that paving bricks usually weather to a different colour from a similar brick used in a wall. You can lay bricks either on edge or flat, provided there are no holes pierced through or indentations, called 'frogs', on either side. If you use bricks flat you tend to see rather more of the basic surface than the pointed joints, which can be a good thing. As with paving slabs, the type of pointing makes a vital difference to the final appearance. Joints that are deeply raked emphasise each module, while flush pointing produces a more uniform surface.

A good paving brick will be 'hard' enough or sufficiently well-fired to withstand frost and can be laid in three basic patterns (see Figure 5.6), each one of which will have repercussions in design terms.

a *Stretcher bond* involves laying bricks in the same pattern as a wall, either flat or on edge. The direction of the courses will, however, give the pattern 'movement' in a particular direction. Bricks laid across a terrace or path tend to make the space feel wider, which can be useful in opening up a narrow area. When bricks are laid running away from a viewpoint they lead the eye on in a specific direction. Soldier courses are a variation of stretcher bond and here the joints coincide, providing a more static composition. Both bonds are easily laid to a camber or cross-fall. A path with a camber has its centre slightly higher than the edges to facilitate drainage.

b *Basketweave* is a traditional pattern and can be laid in groups of three on edge or two flat, each group forming a square. This is perhaps the most static brick paving pattern as the squares give the overall design stability.

c *Herringbone* is a more intricate pattern and you can see it around many historic buildings. Again, the bricks can be laid flat or on edge, either diagonally or at right angles to the overall design. This is a complicated pattern and looks it, the diagonal bond involving cutting at the edges. Having said that, it can be most attractive in an intimate situation, but overpowering in large areas. Bricks are thicker than the average paving slab, so the depth of foundation will have to be adjusted where you are mixing the materials.

Lay bricks on a 5 cm thick dry mortar mix, consisting of four parts soft sand to one part cement, by volume. Once they are in position, brush more dry mortar into the open joints and leave it to set with the aid of water drawn up from the soil by capillary action. If you water

the mortar in there is a danger that the bricks will become stained with cement. Alternatively, you can bed bricks on wet mortar and carefully point the joints. When you do this be particularly careful not to stain the surface. A wire brush will effectively remove dry mortar stains. The beauty of brick paving lies in its texture and pattern, and good workmanship is essential to preserve these qualities.

Stable pavers

These were widely used for surfacing yards and stables and look rather like bars of chocolate, being divided on top into cubes or diamonds. They are normally dark blue and very hard, the dimensions being roughly that of a thin brick. They have much the same character as granite setts, albeit slightly more architectural, but their uneven surface makes them a slightly precarious paving for sitting areas. You can use them for drives and also as strips between other materials such as gravel, tarmac or concrete, where they often provide the ideal link between an older property and its garden.

Timber

Timber decking and steps are widely employed in Scandinavia and America to give a sensible paving that blends into virtually any setting. With our climate the main prerequisite for decking is a good circulation of air passing around the timbers and this means lifting the surface slightly above ground level. On a sloping site this can make a superb arrangement, with decks and steps on different levels. Another advantage is that trees or large plants can be allowed to grow through cut-outs, which looks particularly effective.

Railway sleepers

These solid lengths of timber are virtually indestructible, having been soaked in preservative for years. They can hardly be used as formal paving but have a great air of stability, associating particularly well with planting in an informal part of the garden. They can be used to make raised beds, continuing the theme in a vertical direction, and they also make excellent informal steps. They should be bedded on sand using a simple stretcher bond; their weight makes this a two-man job. Try to avoid cutting them. This is impossible with a hand saw and is really only practical with a power tool. If you are constructing raised beds or steps you can drill the sleepers at either end to accept steel rods which can be driven into the ground.

Log slices

Dutch elm disease in this country has led to there being a great deal of this timber available and it is ideal for a wide range of applications in the garden. If you cut a trunk into slices you can use these as stepping stones through planting or as paving in an informal setting.

Always remove the bark, which holds water and accelerates rot. If you lay the slices through a lawn make sure that they are set just below the level of the turf to allow easy mowing.

What could I use to make a drive or hardstanding area?

Drives and hardstanding areas are often built up from a series of strong, flowing curves, and so you need fluid materials that can take up these shapes without cutting. The other important consideration when you surface large areas is cost, which usually precludes the use of most small paving materials. The obvious man-made material to use is concrete, laid *in situ*, while possible natural materials include gravel and tarmac.

Gravel (see Figure 5.7)

Gravel can be used almost anywhere but often looks best in relation to buildings. It is less formal than paving but more severe than grass, and looks equally at home in a crisp urban setting or around a country cottage.

The use of gravel need not be confined to drives; it can be an excellent alternative to grass in a tiny garden or dark courtyard. Sculptural planting of such species as acanthus, echinops, hostas and fatsia will look particularly fine against such a practical but neutral background.

Thorough preparation is essential at all stages of laying, particularly if traffic will be using the surface. You can avoid that annoying tendency to get a treadmill effect

to the front door if you keep to the correct procedure.

Laying gravel

The prime rule for laying gravel is thorough compaction at all stages of the job and, if you have enough room for one, it can be well worth hiring a vibrating mechanical roller. If the area is cramped use a heavy hand roller of about 500–750 kg. Simple shapes and curves are more easily worked and look better than awkward corners.

If you are laying a drive a really substantial base is necessary. The depth of this depends on site conditions but obviously well-compacted ground that has been consolidated by builders' lorries will need less hardcore than a soft, virgin area. On average you should roll a base of hardcore, crushed stone or clinker to a finished thickness of 10 cm. Top this with gravel that passes through a 5 cm screen, and compact it to a 5 cm thickness, which will fill any gaps in the hardcore and provide an even surface. Next, spread a 2.5 cm layer of fine gravel mixed with hoggin. The latter acts as a bonding agent. (Hoggin is one of those mystical names bandied about by landscape gardeners to confuse clients. It is in fact a clay, usually from the same pit as gravel, that acts as a binder. It should be made wet enough to be worked easily but if it becomes saturated disaster sets in, as it sticks to everything apart from the drive, including tools, boots and rollers – and it is virtually impossible to remove the stains from carpets!)

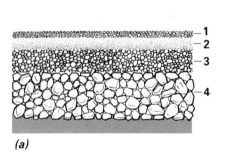
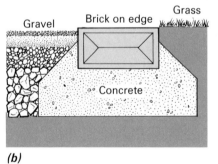
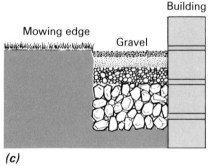

(a) **(b)** **(c)**

(d)

Figure 5.7 Gravel.
(a) Gravel (1) should always be laid on a well-consolidated base, made up of layers of hoggin (2), coarse gravel (3) and hardcore (4).
(b) A neat edge to a gravel drive is essential, bricks set in concrete being ideal. In this case the drive adjoins grass, which is set at a slightly higher level than the brick to allow easy mowing.
(c) Where grass adjoins a building a neat edge of gravel or loose cobbles can separate lawn and building, preventing a mower banging into the wall.
(d) If drainage is a problem in the vicinity of a drive, the insertion of land drains will lower the watertable to an acceptable level.

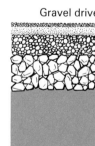
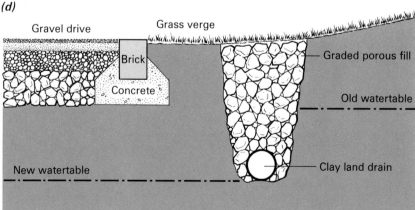

Finally, put on a topdressing of gravel. This should be only about 1.5 cm thick and, if possible, be a local, washed 'pea shingle'. Roll it well in to produce a durable finish and firm surface.

Drainage

Drainage is particularly important in gravel areas as water quickly undermines the surface. If in doubt dig holes on either side of the proposed drive and if the water-table is within 60 cm of the surface lay land drains to remedy the problem (see pp. 36–7).

Edges

The finish to a gravel drive is vital. It is one of the first things you see on entering a property. There are various alternatives:

a Bricks laid on edge, end-to-end, make a fine edge and they should be set in concrete.

b Metal strips are sometimes used but, although this gives a superbly crisp line, it is an expensive operation. (These strips are not to be confused with the dreadful corrugated aluminium edging that is available and looks frightful in virtually any setting.)

c In a rural area a lawn at a slightly higher level can dip down to the drive, being neatly cut back once a year with an edging iron to retain the line. This sort of treatment is the kind of understatement that forms the basis of good garden design.

Tarmac (see Figure 5.8)

There are two tarmac surfaces available, bitumen and asphalt, the latter being more commonly used in domestic situations. Bitumen is hard-wearing and suitable for heavy traffic and its laying is best left to a specialised contractor. The rash of suburban paths and drives, all laid by a particular contractor, with white chippings dotted over the surface, is evidence of the currant bun syndrome which should be avoided like the plague. A similar nasty addition to the street scene are tarmac drives in hues of red and green. These colours are bad enough on a tennis court; in a front garden they are a disaster.

Asphalt and bitumen, although being ideal for free-form drives, can look equally at home contained within a grid of slabs, brick or granite setts and this treatment can help relieve an otherwise somewhat oppressive area. The edges can be retained in the same way as gravel, with brick, timber or metal strips.

You can buy asphalt in bags and easily lay it in your garden. Rake it out over a base of hardcore which has been 'blinded' (covered) with ash. Roll it immediately and apply a suitable topdressing of gravel.

Figure 5.8 Ashpalt or bitumen can be used for paths or drives and both rely on a well-prepared base *(a)*. Such surfaces are ideal in a 'free-form' pattern, but look equally good retained within an 'architectural' framework of slabs, brick or neat wood strips *(b)*.

OTHER FEATURES OF HARD LANDSCAPE

Steps

Inevitably in many garden situations you encounter a change of level. In an informal setting you can deal with this by gentle contouring and flowing lawns, but within a hard landscape area steps are both a necessary and an enjoyable feature.

Steps in a garden should never be mean. Progress up and down them should be leisurely. There is a safe formula for outside steps which states that the risers should be no more than about 15 cm while an ideal tread (the flat part) wants to be approximately 45 cm. As far as width is concerned, there is no set rule, but a wide flight looks more restful and is often easier to negotiate than a narrow stair (see Figure 5.9). If space permits and the flight is long it is often desirable to incorporate a landing every 15 treads or so. This could form a platform for a group of pots or a well chosen statue, while the ensuing steps could change direction, either doubling back or leading off at an angle of 45° or 90°.

Construction can be in any of the materials discussed above. Where stone or pre-cast concrete slabs are used as treads, let them overhang the risers by 2.5–5.0 cm, thus creating a subtle shadow that softens the flight.

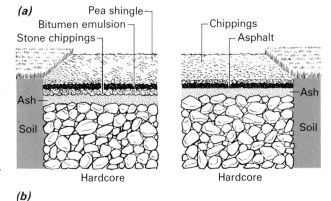

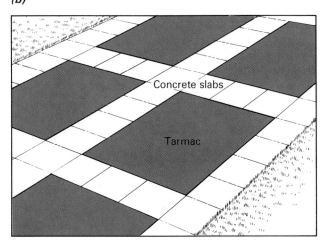

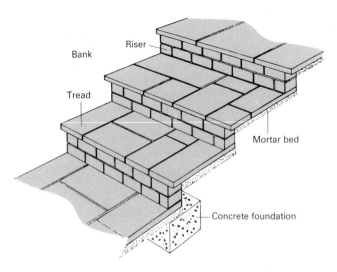

Figure 5.9 Steps in a garden should be as wide and generous as possible. The bottom riser is built up from a concrete foundation, the treads being bedded on mortar. Each successive riser is built off the back of the tread below.

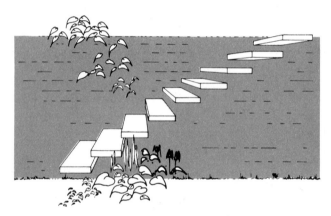

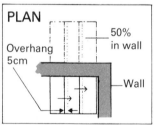

PLAN

Overhang 5cm

50% in wall

Wall

Figure 5.10 Cantilevered steps need at least half of their length buried in the adjoining wall. Each tread should also overhang the next by 5cm. If handled properly they can make a dramatic stair.

You can build unusual steps by cantilevering unsupported treads out from a wall (Figure 5.10) or setting logs across a slope (Figure 5.11). Out of place these would look very gimmicky, but used with care, taking into consideration the overall design and character of an area, the result could be perfect.

Steps need not necessarily occupy only part of a garden. If they are large enough – big circles or overlapping hexagons (Figure 5.12) perhaps – they could virtually fill the whole of a sloping site. The outline could be of brick or

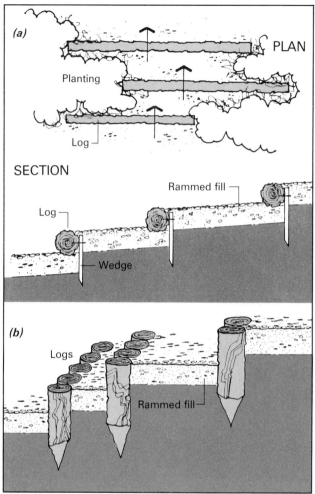

(a) PLAN

Planting

Log

SECTION

Rammed fill

Log

Wedge

(b)

Logs

Rammed fill

Figure 5.11 Logs can make versatile and informal steps. Either place them across the line of a slope, driving wedges in to provide support (a), or drive shorter sections into the ground to produce a slightly more formal flight (b).

stone and the treads could be paving of various kinds, grass, planting or gravel. Such steps almost become terraces, a fact which underlines the point that there is often no demarcation between features in a garden.

Ramps
Steps, of course, are all very well, but if they link every level in a garden it will be virtually impossible to move mowers, barrows or wheeled toys from one area to another. In this case it is sensible to incorporate a ramp or series of slopes that can provide access. Such a feature could be treated architecturally, when virtually any of the preceding materials could be used, or informally. In the latter situation a grass ramp, linking two lawns, can look particularly effective and in many ways forms a softer solution in an informal part of the garden.

Manholes

Inevitably, the problem of manholes rears its head. They are always in the most awkward position, right outside the french windows, usually turned at the most difficult angle that will play havoc with the neat paving pattern you have worked out. What on earth can you do with the wretched things? First of all they are necessary and to concrete or pave over them, although aesthetically pleasing, is not to be recommended. Sooner or later you will need to lift them. Secondly, never place a pot or statue on top: far from detracting from the problem, this simply draws the eye and effectively advertises the presence of a manhole.

It is possible to purchase recessed covers that allow paving to be fitted into them. These, coupled with the fact that the underlying frame can often be reset to align with the surrounding paving, will in most cases solve the problem.

If a manhole can be included within a planted area then it can be disguised effectively and you can build up an attractive composition of spreading plants, cobbles and boulders that will do much to temper the architectural line of surrounding paving.

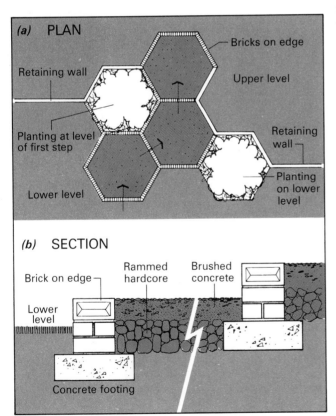

Figure 5.12 *(a)* Large hexagonal or circular steps can occupy a large area. The pattern can be continued to include planted areas and lawn. *(b)* A section through this flight shows a surface of brushed concrete, retained by bricks laid on edge. The infill could be gravel, grass or any small modular material.

Raised beds

These bring the third dimension, height, into play and can be particularly useful. They can fit into the terrace pattern, either defining the edge of the sitting area or occupying part of a grid pattern within the overall design. Such beds should echo materials used in the vicinity and can be built to various heights. Not only does this give young plants an appearance of greater maturity but it makes cultivation a great deal easier – an important point to bear in mind for older or disabled gardeners.

Another advantage is that you can choose the soil type in a raised bed and this might allow you to grow specialised plants. Remember that such a bed is, in effect, a large flower pot, needing drainage holes and regular watering during any dry weather.

CHECKPOINT

Now that you have read this chapter you should recognise the importance of hard landscape in your garden design and have made sure that you have allocated enough space for hard surfaces on your scale plan. You should also be able to recognise how the characteristics of different materials determine their use and be able to choose those materials most suited to your situation and design ideas. To check that you have understood the points made in this chapter, answer the following questions.

1. What minimum size of paved area should you aim at for the following:
   a a sitting area;
   b paths;
   c hardstanding?
2. What two criteria can you use to help you choose materials for hard surfaces?
3. At what gradient should hard surfaces fall away from a building?
4. How would you point between paving slabs to emphasise each one?
5. What is the function of expansion joints?
6. What kind of material could you use as a pedestrian deterrent?
7. What is the prime rule for laying gravel?
8. What is the best type of material to use for a path up to the front door of a red brick, terraced house with a small front garden:
   a cobbles;
   b gravel;
   c paving bricks to match the house;
   d concrete slabs?
   You could use a combination of these.
9. How and why do you 'cure' concrete?
10. How could you edge a gravel drive, bordered by flower beds, in an inexpensive way?

Check your answers against the information given in the chapter.

As was explained in Chapter 5, soft landscape is the planted area which, along with hard landscape, 'fills in' your garden design; soft landscape puts the flesh on the bones of your composition and is made up of the following components.

a *Planting* (see Chapter 7) wraps the garden about in vegetation and can provide space division in certain situations. However, it will occupy only a portion of the total ground area you want to cover. A larger amount may be covered by

b *Lawns*, but beware of the common practice of simply slapping grass down where nothing else exists. An alternative might be to use

c *Ground-covering plants* which are available in a wide range of species that will give you colour and interest throughout the year and are easy to maintain.

Planting is discussed in detail in Chapter 7. In this chapter I will look at the place of lawns in a garden design, their shape, construction and maintenance, and the choice of plants for ground cover.

LAWNS

What is the function of a lawn in a garden design?

Lawns quite simply pull things together, as in any garden there is a great deal of separate activity and interest engendered elsewhere. This would include patio, flower beds, vegetable garden, sheds, greenhouse as well as hardstanding and storage of various kinds. A lawn is the common denominator that forms a restful backdrop, stabilising the overall composition as well as providing room for a host of other family activities.

How can I keep a lawn looking the way it should?

A lawn should suit your needs, not the other way round! For the average family with boisterous children and pets, a utility surface is all you can expect or need. In fact, a sprinkling of daisies and the addition of the gem-like speedwell adds immeasurably to the overall sward of green. Far too much time and money is spent on trying to keep utility lawns looking like bowling greens. Only in the case of the specialist is this amount of effort justified.

What is the best shape for a lawn in my small garden?

Look at the basic shapes you marked on your garden plan. The lawn may well be the largest of these and its shape will follow the pattern that you decided was best suited to your garden, perhaps consisting of strong rectangles or curves. These work very well in an intimate setting, increasing the feeling of space rather than detracting from it. It is quite wrong to try to scale down the sweeping lines of a landscape park. All that you end up with is a meaningless jumble. This is what led to the demise of the Victorian garden, which imitated the grander affairs of Brown and Repton in a smaller area.

Finally, avoid small patches or triangles of lawn: they are difficult to mow and simply appear 'fussy'.

Should the lawn have different levels in my small garden?

If you have a small garden that slopes it is not worth creating different levels before you lay a lawn. A sloping lawn that flows down a small garden is altogether more restful and easier to cut than a series of different levels which look uneasy.

Constructing a lawn

Whether you use seed or turf for your lawn depends on a number of factors, such as the quality of lawn you wish to make, how quickly you want it, and how much money you want to spend. Methods of preparation and laying vary as do the seasons at which work is best carried out.

Turf

In many respects turf provides an almost instant lawn. It is quick to lay and quick to establish, which make it a sensible choice in a small, family garden where grass is needed as a play space. However, the quality of turf varies greatly and if possible you should ask to see a sample before you buy. The quality control of meadow turf has been a traditional stumbling block. The term 'meadow turf' is still quoted by contractors and advertisements and can turn out to be either old pasture with a good mixture of perennial weeds and coarse grasses, or specially seeded land. It is possible now for turf to be grown to far higher specifications and it is available, although at a higher cost, in large rolls, rather like a carpet. Whatever the quality, the turf should have been treated against weeds before lifting, but it is worth bearing in mind that even if a lawn is weed-free initially, invasion by seeds, particularly in a rural area, is almost inevitable.

What is the best time of year to lay turf?
You can lay turf at virtually any time of the year, providing the ground is not completely waterlogged, solid with frost, or baked dust-dry. Before turf-laying, though, the ground must be prepared by thorough cultivating and grading (removing surface irregularities). As you do this, incorporate any organic material or fertiliser.

When your turf arrives it should have plenty of roots and look green. Do not leave it in a stack for more than a couple of days as it quickly deteriorates and goes yellow.

What equipment do I need for laying turves?
Make sure you have the following equipment: a wheelbarrow to bring turves in; rake; spade; half-moon edging iron for trimming up; scaffold boards; pegs, if the lawn is to slope steeply.

How do I lay turves?
Work off the scaffold boards and put the turves down like bricks in a wall, using a simple stretcher bond so that the joints do not coincide. Butt the sections together closely and lightly tamp them down to provide an even surface. If you are working on a relatively steep slope push wooden pegs through the surface until new roots have grown away. If the weather is dry make sure you provide ample irrigation from a sprinkler. If the turf does dry out and shrink, leaving open joints, brush in sifted soil to fill the gaps and water it in. This watering will be particularly important.

Keep off the new grass for as long as possible; a minimum of two to three weeks is sensible.

Seed
Select your seed mix carefully as it is the choice of mix that determines the finish of your lawn. You can introduce fine or coarse grasses as well as mixtures that are tolerant of shady conditions, which are useful under trees or in an orchard area.

The initial preparation of the ground is a little more critical than for turf (see below) and the lawn will take longer to establish, which might well be important in a family situation.

Seed is much cheaper to use than turf, particularly for large areas. Also, because it was carefully selected in the first place, it may be cheaper to maintain as there should only be a minimum number of weeds.

What is the best time of year to sow seed?
The two main seasons for sowing seed are spring and late summer or early autumn. This timing itself can be restrictive, but in the final analysis, if you want a near-perfect end result, seed will be your natural choice.

How do I prepare the ground for sowing?
To grow a successful lawn you need a minimum of 10 cm of topsoil. If the lawn is to be sown in spring, preparation should be carried out in the previous autumn; if you are sowing in the autumn, prepare the ground during the spring.

Remove all stones over 2.5 cm in diameter, including builders' rubble, bits of metal and any other debris. Stones less than 2.5 cm can be left, as these are ideal to improve drainage. Any root or perennial weeds should be eliminated, either by hand or by using a chemical weed-killer. This will involve thorough cultivation and raking.

Once the ground is clear it must be graded to the required levels, eliminating any humps and depressions that will prevent satisfactory mowing. At this stage check that the depth of topsoil is sufficient and tread all over the lawn area to firm loose soil down.

A final job will be the application of a pre-seed fertiliser at the rate of 100–140 g/m².

Looking after a lawn

Edges
The way in which a lawn abuts other areas of the garden is important and can continue a theme from one place to another as well as having a considerable influence on maintenance.

One of the perpetual chores on many lawns is edge clipping and over the years numerous manual and power tools have been introduced to ease the burden. In fact you can virtually eliminate the task if you introduce a mowing edge. This takes the form of a path, made from courses of brick, stone or other materials, that divides grass from planting. (Be sure that the paving is at least 1.5 cm below the lawn so that mower blades run smoothly over the top.) It is then necessary to trim up the edge only once a year with a spade or, better still, a half-moon edging iron. Another advantage is that mower and planting are kept entirely separate and that annoying tendency to mow off flowers and foliage is eliminated.

Another awkward point is where grass runs right up to a building or paving at a higher level and you see an untidy strip of grass that the mower is unable to reach. Brick or stone would again provide an effective edge, as would a neat division of loose cobbles or gravel, set at a slightly lower level.

Lawn-mowers
Over the last few years lawn-mowers have been developed out of all recognition, as the battle between the cylinder and hover machines bears testimony. There was a time when the only choice was between a heavy hand machine and an expensive motor mower. Today we have a vast range that can be powered by petrol or electricity, and most of which can tackle slopes and lengths of grass that were hitherto impossible to cut with ease. Having said

that, it is obviously impractical to have a garden constructed entirely around steep slopes and a combination of retaining walls – gently sloping lawns and grass or planted banks will probably be called for.

Hover mowers can handle steep banks but remember that the transition between sloping and horizontal surfaces should be smooth, otherwise there will be a point at the bottom that the blades are unable to reach. Flat surfaces can be cut with any of the standard types of mower, cylinder, hover or rotary. When you use a cylinder mower remember that it will produce the traditional 'striped' effect which will affect the design inasmuch as the lines will draw the eye. In cultural terms it is not advisable to cut a lawn always in the same direction, but the line you take will certainly have a bearing on the overall pattern.

Drainage

The fact that grass is a plant means that good drainage encourages healthy development. Waterlogging limits root growth and the presence of moss is almost invariably an indication of this. Without going into the details of turf maintenance, suffice it to say that it is sensible to keep a lawn well aerated; in extreme cases it may be necessary to lay land drains to remove excess moisture.

Rough grass

In a larger-size garden there is no need for smoothly mown lawns to extend to the furthest corners. It can be most effective to leave areas of rougher grass, naturalised with bulbs and wild flowers. These need be cut only occasionally with a rotary machine and are ideal under

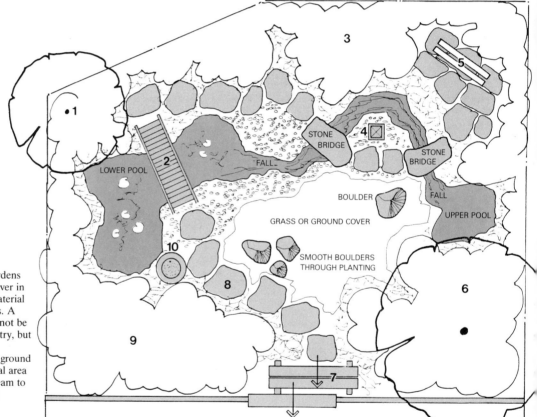

Figure 6.1 Japanese gardens rely heavily on ground cover in the form of both plant material and loose stone chippings. A true Japanese garden cannot be created outside that country, but the style can certainly be translated. In this garden ground cover is used in the central area around the pools and stream to form a carpet of differing textures.

PLANTING LIST

KEY TO PLAN
1 Silver birch
2 Bridge
3 Mixed shrub planting
4 Statue
5 Seat
6 Mixed shrub planting
7 Timber steps
8 Stepping stones
9 Mixed shrubs
10 Stone lantern

2 *Helleborus corsicus*
1 *Hebe* 'Great Orme'
1 *Choisya ternata*
2 *Fatsia japonica* 'Variegata'
3 *Hedera helix* 'Glacier'
1 *Viburnum plicatum* 'Mariesii'
3 *Anemone japonica* (white)
2 *Euphorbia wulfenii*
5 *Ligularia* 'Sungold'
2 *Arundinaria murielae*
4 *Astilbe* 'Fanale'
1 *Philadelphus* 'Beauclerk'

1 *Clematis tangutica*
2 *Hydrangea macrophylla* 'Blue Wave'
1 *Cornus alba* 'Elegantissima'
5 *Lysichitum americanum*
2 *Cytisus × kewensis*
4 *Hosta fortunei* 'Picta'
4 *Arundinaria viridistriata*
30 *Festuca glauca*
3 *Viburnum davidii*
2 *Pieris taiwanensis*
2 *Arundinaria nitida*
8 *Sarcococca hookeriana* 'Digyna'
1 *Spirea × arguta*

1 *Hedera canariensis* 'Gloire de Merengo'
5 *Primula* 'Ashore hybrids'
7 *Hosta sieboldiana*
2 *Deutzia scabra* 'Plena'
1 *Arundinaria japonica*
2 *Spirea × bumalda* 'Anthony Waterer'
1 *Clematis macropetala*
3 *Skimmia japonica* 'Foremanii'
3 *Sasa veitchii*
50 *Ajuga reptans* 'Atropurpurea'
45 *Pachysandra terminalis*
10 *Avena candida*
1 *Rheum palmatum*

fruit trees or as a link with the larger landscape in a rural setting. Formal paths would be out of place here, but a mown path that weaves in and out of trees and informal planting, terminating at a summer house or arbour would be delightful. Mowing need take place only three or four times a year, coinciding with the dieback of spring bulbs, the seed formation of wild flowers, and the aftermath of autumn crocuses (colchicums), with a final cut before winter sets in.

On a grand scale fine lawns give way to rough grass which dips into a ha-ha that leads the eye towards a horizon.

Chamomile lawn

If you have only a very small garden and do not get time to cut grass regularly try growing the traditional chamomile lawn. It does not accept heavy wear but it is delightfully fragrant when crushed by the occasional footfall. It enjoys a sunny spot, needs no cutting and knits together to form a fine carpet. Do remember, though, that such a lawn cannot be treated with weedkiller, and any weeds that appear will have to be removed by hand. A small chamomile lawn is charming; a larger one can create a lot of work! Chamomile is, in fact, one form of plant ground cover, the subject of the next, and last, section of this chapter.

GROUND COVER

Generally, ground cover is a low-growing, dense and preferably evergreen mat of plants and is used as a carpet to exclude weed growth beneath taller shrubs and herbaceous material. However, shrubs have a drooping or horizontal habit that produces their own cover by excluding light and preventing weed growth. *Viburnum plicatum* 'Mariesii', *Mahonia aquifolium* (Oregon grape) and such large junipers as *J. pfitzeriana* or *J. × media* 'Hetzii' are excellent examples of this.

Traditional ground cover

In many ways grass is the ultimate ground cover, producing uniformity over a wide area. Normally, however, we think of more colourful material, the effective use of which relies heavily on the historical influence of Japanese gardens (see Figure 6.1) and, more recently, such great landscape architects as the Brazilian Burle Marx. In this sort of planting you look at the overall effect rather than the individual characteristics of a plant. With care you can build up subtle relationships with, say, the low mounds of *Festuca glauca* (grey sheep's fescue grass) contrasting with the larger felty leaves of sage, *Salvia officinalis* 'Purpurascens' (the colour break of purple and grey is particularly effective), or the delicate dew-filled

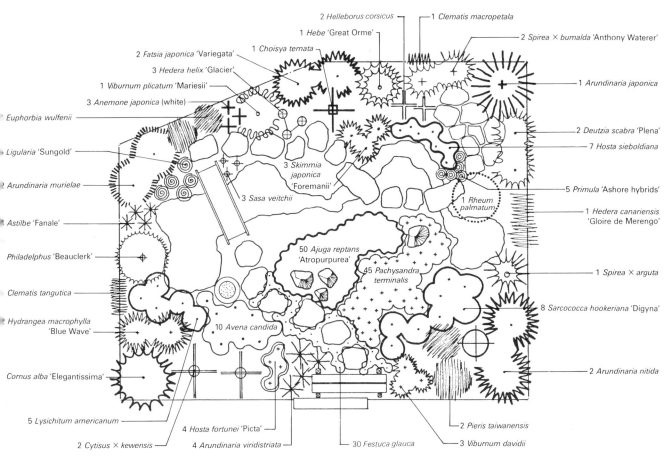

leaves of *Alchemilla mollis* (lady's mantle) seen against the taller leaves and flowers of pale pink astilbe (spiraea), both ideal set against the backdrop of water.

The introduction of accent plants such as yucca (Spanish bayonet), phormium (New Zealand flax) or acanthus (bear's breech) will be a dramatic foil to low ground cover, while to echo the latter with smooth boulders and loose cobbles adds to the dimension.

Remember to have a look at plants with a fresh eye, in the same way as you considered paving materials. Many climbers can also run along the ground, although they will leap up a wall or tree at the first opportunity. Honeysuckle and ivy are excellent examples of this, the former having the added bonus of fragrant flowers. In fact both of these are found in the wild state and in consequence naturalise easily into woodland or an orchard garden.

What ground cover can I use in a small garden?

While large areas of ground cover obviously fit well into a broader composition, heathers and conifers may be ideal in a more intimate situation. Heathers can provide colour and interest throughout the year, and the vast range of colour, form and accent of conifers acts as an ideal foil, as long as they are used in moderation with an eye to their effect on the overall group.

How does ground cover spread?

Ground cover spreads either by runners above or below ground or by groups of similar plants knitting together. While the growth of the latter can be estimated with some degree of accuracy, as one knows the ultimate approximate height and spread, the extent of 'running' plants is almost unlimited. This can be an excellent characteristic in certain situations – ivy under trees for example – but it can become a plague in others, as more delicate material is likely to be over-run. In this eventuality keep a close eye on development and do not hesitate to cut back the more rampant material when necessary.

It is this rampant nature of many ground-covering plants which makes many people dubious about using them. It is allied to the old question of what constitutes a weed. A weed is simply a plant growing in the wrong place. *Hypericum calycinum* (St John's wort) and *Lamium galeobdolon* (dead nettle) are often considered weeds, as once established they are almost impossible to eradicate. Used in the right place, however – the hypericum as a carpet on a sun-drenched bank or the lamium in almost impossible shade – they can provide a fine display, reducing maintenance to an absolute minimum. As with all aspects of planting design and selection, *choose a plant for the job you want it to do*. The habit of accepting cast-offs from friends, although attractive, can be a recipe for disaster.

In certain situations ground-covering plants can be kept apart or prevented from invading specific areas by a physical barrier such as a path or edging strip of some kind. Alternatively, low-growing shrubs such as skimmia, sarcococca or *Cotoneaster microphyllus* would do a similar but softer-looking job.

Annual ground cover

All the plants I have discussed so far are, of course, either shrubs or hardy perennials, but do not forget that annual species such as salvias, petunias and stocks in the form of carpet bedding can also act as very effective ground covers for a summer season. The Victorian or municipal park formal bedding schemes are one way of handling such material, the serried ranks of bloom having a rigid and architectural line. A more contemporary method is to use drifts of plants that can be hand-sown and thinned out as they start to develop, a far cheaper and faster solution than growing on and pricking out or simply buying boxes of bedding, which is particularly expensive on a large scale. Such a treatment is ideal in a developing border where you need to fill gaps between shrubs and herbaceous material.

CHECKPOINT

Now that you have read this chapter you should have decided on the relative proportions of plants, lawn and ground cover which will make up the soft landscape in your garden. You should also have decided what shape your lawn should be to fit into the overall pattern of your garden, what quality of finish is suited to your needs, and whether you will use turf or seed to construct your lawn. Finally, you should be able to choose ground-covering plants according to the jobs you want them to do. To check that you have fully understood the points made in this chapter, answer the following questions.

1 What is the advantage of including ground-covering plants in your soft landscape?
2 How are areas of lawn used in a garden design?
3 Which shapes should you use for a lawn if you want to increase the feeling of space in a small garden?
4 What is meant by 'meadow turf'?
5 Would you use turf or seed if you wanted a high-quality lawn?
6 What can you do to minimise the need to clip the edges of your lawn and at the same time continue a theme in your garden design?
7 Name two shrubs which perform the same function as ground-covering plants.
8 Which ground-covering plants are most suitable for a small garden?
9 Why would you be unlikely to grow *Hypericum calycinum* or *Lamium galeobdolon* in a small garden?
10 Name two annuals that can be used for ground cover.

Check your answers against the information given in the chapter.

The ultimate outside room; old York stone and brick, barbecue and built-in seating with the overhead beams casting light shade. The slight change of level is sensibly handled and planting softens the architectural line of the walls.

Raised bed, railway sleepers as paving and planting combine to form the ideal outdoor room. The fence is built from second-hand timber, the vertical line adding height to the composition.

Dartington Hall in Devon (right) has an excellent example of the sculptural use of earth shaping. Steep grass banks separate terraces while the clipped yew trees introduce a note of drama. Such banks are a maintenance problem and could only be cut with a hover mower.

The link between garden and landscape in a rural situation should be minimal. Here an old fence allows the eye to run on to the fields beyond, drawing them into the overall composition.

This tiny London garden (below) has been floored with old York stone that fades into the surrounding planting. The overhead beams cast light shade and also effectively block the views from neighbours' upstairs windows.

The simple horizontal boards of this fence echo the clean lines of the raised pool below. The shallow step is clearly marked with bricks turned at an angle to the main paving pattern while the statue and plants add interest to the composition.

65

Raised beds and brick paving; the two levels are linked by planting. Notice how African marigolds and Marguerite daisies, both used as annuals, bring 'instant colour' to this setting.

Concrete block pavers, gravel and planting combine in this formal composition. The pool is perfectly constructed and the stepping stones are set on brick piers so that they appear to float just above the water surface.

Gardens during construction always look severe. Broad brick steps drop down past the shell of a pool to a sitting area on the bottom level. See how the top step has been designed to run off the corner of the building, thus tying house and garden together.

Cobbles laid in courses produce a broadly linear pattern.

Good design is never contrived and often natural. This is really a blend of architecture and garden, the solid stone steps leading the eye up from the random stone paving. A hydrangea softens the flight.

Timber decking, provided it has ample ventilation beneath, makes an ideal patio surface. Second-hand timber can be utilised and in this setting the composition has a slightly Japanese feel.

This is a dramatic flight of steps, built from York stone. It has landings every so often and the flight disappears into the planting with a slight air of mystery.

Shrubs and herbaceous material are woven together to provide colour and interest throughout the year. The background of shrubs offers screening and support; hardy perennials bring flowers and delicacy.

This ground cover has reduced maintenance to an absolute minimum. It is a combination of *Hypericum calycinum* and heathers.

This simple brick mowing edge eliminates that chore of hand edging. The turf is set slightly higher than the bricks and an annual trim round with a half-moon edging iron keeps the lawn immaculate.

Ground cover at Arlington Court in Devon (below), a superb arrangement of heights, colours and textures. Maintenance here is reduced to a very low level indeed.

The White Garden at Sissinghurst shows just how effective the use of a single colour can be. Foliage shape, colour and texture are vital ingredients here while the brick path leads the eye towards the arch and yet another 'garden room'.

Planting in this border is designed within a single colour range, purple, pink, pale yellow and that great harmoniser, grey. Much of this planting is herbaceous material and would die down in winter, but the effect is superb during the summer.

Not only are railway sleepers immensely strong but they bring an air of stability to a situation. In this clever water feature, designed by students of Merrist Wood College, the great leaves of *Rheum palmatum* enhance the picture.

Why should potting benches be boring? This corner of the garden is a feature in itself and thoroughly practical too. Pots and planting soften the outline while a bold-leaved ivy climbs up one side.

Seats need not always be bought off the peg. Why not build one into a garden? This seat wraps itself around a raised pool, the wall beneath being painted black to soften the line with shadow. Brick paving here is laid in a simple stretcher bond, notice how it dies off in a random pattern into the planting at the far end.

This old stone paving has started to break and in so doing has provided ideal growing conditions for low, spreading plants. The superb old lead tank proves how much better is the real thing than fibreglass imitations.

Hostas make ideal tub plants and this no-nonsense half barrel is the perfect foil for such sculptural leaves. Note also the textures of paving, brick and stone combining with water and a raised bed built from railway sleepers.

Statues can be grand or subtle. This one makes a bold statement and the broad leaves of *Vitis coignetiae*, together with the dramatic flowers of acanthus, help to emphasise the overall pattern.

Rock is used in two ways here. Outcrops are set as 'sculpture' against the skyline and the stream is a relaxed and very natural feature. The heavy background planting of rhododendron acts as a foil to yellow azaleas, and a ground cover of *Hebe pinguifolia* 'Pagei' sweeps along the front of the border providing continuity and offering low maintenance.

Summer-houses and garden buildings are often far too stereotyped. This is a modern style, built from concrete blocks and having a timber fascia that echoes the timber decking of the terrace. Broad timber steps drop down the change of level and stepping stones cross the stream that flows into a natural pond.

A garden seat on this scale doubles as a table and play surface. It also positively ties the tree into the surrounding paving pattern.

Every garden needs a secret corner and this simple arbour provides the perfect sitting area. Old-fashioned planting with climbing roses, hollyhocks, fuchsia and a vine provide a softly modelled picture.

Remember that the garden has to cater for the ugly as well as the attractive. This simply but carefully detailed bin store blends well into the paved area, the ivy dropping down from a higher level.

A statue should always have a place to go and should never be just slapped down anywhere. This bust has been positioned precisely within the angle of the wall, the broad leaves of *Fatsia japonica* being the perfect foil.

Simplicity is the key to good design and this seat is built from four pieces of solid stone.

Overhead beams and all garden features should be carefully detailed and built. See how these beams have been left square at the ends which gives them a crisp, unfussy appearance.

This small garden pool blends well into the surrounding paving. The coping just overhangs the water, casting a shadow, and note the sensible planting of waterside species.

CHAPTER SEVEN

Plants and planting design

Geographical location/Microclimate/Planting design
Ground preparation/Checkpoint

Up until now you have been looking at your garden in social and architectural terms. You have planned the distribution of various features, taking into account your personality and needs, and you have used all the components of 'hard landscape' to create the framework or skeleton that holds your overall composition together. You have also begun to 'fill in' your composition with two components of soft landscape – lawns and ground cover. However, it is the third component of soft landscape, planting, which will really bring your garden to life. Plants are developing organisms, and although holding a conversation with them is perhaps unrealistic you can certainly relate to flowers and foliage rather better than to bricks and mortar. This should not detract from the latter – in fact it makes the underlying design especially important – but it does mean that you should make sure that the hard and soft elements within your garden work together.

How soon can I buy plants?
In much the same way as you refrained from putting pen to paper too soon in working out a design, so you must resist the urge to rush out and buy the first plants you see in a garden centre. This is because first you must consider three factors which affect your choice of plants:
a where you live;
b what your microclimate is like;
c planting design and the way to build up a pattern in your garden.

GEOGRAPHICAL LOCATION
Broadly speaking, the location of your garden in geographical terms will determine what you can grow. Tender plants will not survive hard winters and this can eliminate many species from a proposed planting plan. Seaside conditions, salt spray and high winds are other limiting factors, although the influence of a warm current such as the Gulf Stream provides unusually temperate conditions along the west coast of Scotland. Just inland the effect is lost altogether.
● Visit your local garden centre or contact your local horticultural society to seek advice on the types of plant most suitable for your location and any which you should avoid because of local weather patterns.

MICROCLIMATE
I discussed features of microclimate in Chapter 1 and you marked on your site plan any areas of your garden affected by wind, frost, etc. In this section I will look at microclimate again and suggest which plants you should, and should not, grow under the various conditions.

Wind
Wind can be a real problem and bearing in mind the cost of erecting a wall or permeable screen, tough shrubs such as *Prunus laurocerasus*, *Viburnum rhytidophyllum*, *Viburnum tinus* and *Elaeagnus × ebbingei* can provide an effective answer, their branches breaking the main force while creating minimal turbulence (see Figure 7.1). Such planting provides shelter for the garden as an outside room and also the colourful, more delicate material positioned in its lee. As a general rule a screen of plants, whether trees or shrubs, can provide an area of shelter in a lateral direction of up to ten times their height. The stronger the wind, the more gently the break should be graded, lower-growing species being positioned in front of taller material so that the wind climbs in a sweep rather than coming to a full stop.

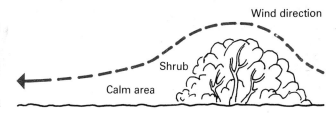

Figure 7.1 A semi-permeable screen of tough shrub planting produces calm conditions on the leeward side for several times the height of the screen itself in a longitudinal direction.

Shade
Many gardeners despair of shady conditions, thinking that most plants must have an open, sunny aspect to flourish. You have only to look at the natural environment to see how wrong this is.

Trees are the main element casting shade in the

countryside, but in a garden there are the additional problems of buildings, fences, walls and established shrubs. It is worth bearing in mind that the amount of sunlight over a given area varies not only with the daily passage of the sun across the sky but also with the time of year. Shadows in winter are far longer than in summer.

Depending on the particular element casting shade, the ground conditions will also vary. Large trees and shrubs remove water and nourishment from an area, while a house wall with overhanging eaves provides a desert below. Climbers should therefore always be positioned at least 15 cm away from a house wall and trained in from that point, so that their young roots will be able to gather more moisture.

What can I grow in shady areas?

Foliage rather than flower is the answer in shade and some shade-tolerant plants have bold, handsome leaves, e.g. *Fatsia japonica*, *Viburnum rhytidophyllum* and the mahonias which are good examples of shrubs. Hostas (plantain lilies), bergenias (elephant's ears) and hellebores echo this characteristic at a lower herbaceous level.

Frost

Frost at a microclimatic level is rather different from broad geographical differences in temperature because local variations are often the exception to national climatic trends. In a garden you can soon get to know the pockets where frost forms. You can sometimes eliminate these by opening up a gap in a boundary to allow the cold air to drain away, but if this is impossible be careful to avoid using tender plants in such areas.

An unavoidable problem is the occasional very hard winter, when temperatures drop well below the expected average. In this case tender subjects and hardy varieties alike are affected as the ground becomes frozen solid to a considerable depth. Some plants, and trees in particular, may have a delayed reaction to such damage, often coming into leaf the following spring only to die later in the year. Do not be too hasty to remove seemingly dead frost-damaged plants; very often they can be pruned back to ground level from where new vigorous shoots will appear.

Pollution

Your garden may be affected by three types of pollution – chemical, audible and visual.

Chemical pollution. Some shrub species are better suited to urban conditions than others: *Prunus lusitanica* (Portugal laurel), fatsia (finger aralia) and privet (which makes an excellent shrub) are good examples of evergreen material. Conifers, however, are particularly susceptible to chemical pollution, their small leaves becoming quickly clogged with debris.

Noise is becoming an increasing nuisance, but can be greatly reduced by a dense screen of planting. If the intervening ground can be mounded or contoured and then planted, the results will be even better.

Visual pollution really amounts to a bad view and I have already considered how this can be screened by the judicious use of plants, or the inclusion of an attractive sight line. Within the visual pollution category you can include oil tanks, ugly garages, dustbin stores and sheds. Where it is impractical or impossible to screen these at a distance, a suitable climber might be trained over or around them. Russian vine (*Polygonum baldschuanicum*) is aptly nicknamed 'mile a minute' and does an excellent job in a short time, having the bonus of huge sprays of creamy white flowers. Large-leaved ivies, evergreen honeysuckle and *Clematis montana* are also useful in this respect.

● Note on your scale plan, against any areas you've marked as being affected by wind, shade, etc., which plants you might grow in these areas. This will be useful when you come to make your planting plan (see below).

PLANTING DESIGN

I need a finished garden quickly. How long will it take?

So often you hear of the wish to create an instant garden and this question of a time-scale is crucial to landscape design. You can, of course, mass plants so that they knit together more quickly but in many ways this is wasteful, as thinning out is inevitable in the long run. A better solution is to interplant slower-growing species with fast-maturing types. Broom, buddleia and the mallow *Lavatera olbia* 'Rosea' are ideal in such a situation, as these are comparatively short-lived, and you can remove them as the long-term species fill out and knit together. As a rough guide, a garden planted with standard nursery stock needs at least five years to develop to a point where the overall concept in three dimensions starts to work properly.

How do you work out a planting plan?

For this you will need your scale plan, circles of various sizes on transparent templates and some tracing paper. Read through the remainder of this chapter and as you do so plan your planting as follows:

● In the following instructions I shall refer to 'eventual size'. Remember that this may well be affected by your microclimate: harsh conditions may stunt growth, while a mild environment will encourage growth and increase the eventual proportions.

a Check the eventual size and spread of a selected species and reduce it to the scale of your plan.

b Select a circle of this size and draw it on to tracing paper.

c Lay the tracing paper over your plan and transfer the circle.

d Continue for other species.

As you proceed you can see how much space is occupied and how much is still available and choose your plants accordingly.

Selecting plants

When you look at the plants in your garden centre you may not understand their names and wonder why common names can't be used. The problem with common names is simply that they are inconsistent: what may commonly be called 'hawthorn' in one part of the country is termed 'bread and cheese tree' and 'holy innocents' in other areas. And knowing that a certain shrub is, say, a cotoneaster is still not enough, as *Cotoneaster dammeri* is a ground-covering species while *Cotoneaster* 'Cornubia' can be well over 3 m high.

Plants are classified by botanists to a set system, adopted by horticulturists and nurseries throughout the world. By adhering to this practice you should be able to obtain exactly what you want, whether it be in Macclesfield, Florence or Timbuctoo.

Botanical names are made up as follows.

Family. All plants are grouped into families. The plants within one family have a basic similarity. Dahlias, chrysanthemums and asters, for instance, all belong to the daisy family, Compositae. Look at their flowers and you will notice that they consist of a central disc of minute flowers, surrounded by a ring of showy petals (although on double varieties the central disc has been replaced by even more large petals).

Genus (plural: genera). The genus is the next category down from the family. Every plant is given a generic name, e.g. *Dahlia, Nicotiana, Helleborus*. Such names are usually written in italic with an initial capital letter, although when used singly like this, they may also be written in Roman script with no capital letter.

Species. The plant species is indicated by a 'specific epithet' which is tacked on to the genus. It is rather like the plant's Christian name, e.g. *Nicotiana affinis*. Specific epithets are written in lower case italics and combine with the generic name to describe the plant species.

Varieties. Plant species will occasionally give rise to a peculiar form which is known as a variety. Such a plant is described as follows: *Mahonia repens rotundifolia*, the varietal name being written in lower case italics, after the specific epithet.

Cultivars. Varieties that do not occur naturally, and which are the result of man's intervention, are known as cultivars (cultivated varieties) and these are usually given English names written as follows: *Rhododendron kaempferi* 'Highlight'. They are always placed in single quotation marks with an initial capital letter.

Hybrids. When two distinct species within one genus are 'crossed' to produce a plant that inherits characteristics from both parents, this hybridisation is indicated with a cross, hence *Cistus × corbariensis*. This sun rose is a cross between *Cistus populifolius* and *Cistus salviifolius*.

Bigeneric hybrids. Hybrids made from crossing different genera (always within the same family) are rare, but one in particular is commonly encountered in gardens: × *Cupressocyparis leylandii* (a cross between *Cupressus macrocarpa* and *Chamaecyparis nootkatensis*). Here the plant is given a generic name comprising half of each of its parent's generic names, and preceded by a cross to indicate that the cross was made at generic, not specific, level.

Initially this system of classification seems complicated but it is, in fact, extremely logical and simple to use. As with most things, practice aids perfection, and once you have mastered the system you will find it certainly pays dividends when you are selecting plants for your garden.

How many plants of each species should I include?

With the selection of species you should consider the number of plants in an eventual group. One of the failings of many gardens is the inclusion of too many individual specimens. While this may provide a horticultural paradise it engenders visual chaos, as the overall composition becomes confused and inherently 'busy'. A far better solution is to use plants in groups and drifts of, say, three or four in a small garden and eight or ten in a more spacious situation. Such groups can also reinforce the underlying pattern, sweeping around a curve or emphasising a rectangle.

At last you are ready to consider which plants are best suited to you and your garden and to begin to build up a pattern that will provide colour and interest throughout the year as well as keeping maintenance to whatever level you require. Two planting plans are shown in Figures 7.2 and 7.3.

In the natural landscape you can see planting in distinct layers: forest trees give way to smaller varieties, which in turn drop down to shrubs and finally ground cover. In a garden you can and should adhere to the same broad principles, although you will be using a wider spectrum of material.

To develop your pattern you must use once again the principles of 'hard' and 'soft' landscape. Just as hard landscape was used to provide the bones of your overall garden pattern, so you must create a framework of tough, predominantly evergreen, shrubs to provide screening, shelter and a protective backdrop to a second stage of filling in with lighter, more colourful material. I will talk about each in turn.

Creating a framework
Shrubs

You can begin to select your shrubs using the notes you have already made on your scale plan as to which ones are most suitable in windy or shady areas, and so on.

While many of the shrubs most suitable for your framework have relatively insignificant flowers, their foliage is far from dull. *Viburnum rhytidophyllum* with deeply veined, leathery leaves; *Prunus lusitanica* with shining dark green foliage; *Viburnum tinus*, another evergreen

Figure 7.2 Ground plan (below) and planting plan (right) for a front garden with shared pedestrian and vehicular access which uses planting to reduce maintenance to a minimum. A small chamomile lawn acts as a centrepiece on one side, the heathers on the other. The framework 'skeleton shrubs' are underlined.

PLANTING LIST

A *Erica carnea* 'Myretoun Ruby'
B *Erica carnea* 'Purple Beauty'
C *Erica carnea* 'Springwood White'
D *Calluna vulgaris* 'Robert Chapman'
PERGOLA
1 *Clematis montana* 'Alexander'
2 *Clematis macropetala*

4 *Stachys lanata*
1 *Choisya ternata*
4 *Bergenia cordifolia*
3 *Festus glauca*
3 *Lavandula augustifolia* 'Vera'
3 *Rosmarinus officinalis* 'Miss Jessop's Variety'
1 *Hypericum patulum* 'Hidcote'
6 *Stachys lanata*

2 *Ribes sanguineum*
2 *Senecio greyi*
2 *Cytisus scoparius* 'Goldfinch'
1 *Yucca flaccida*
1 *Choisya ternata*
3 *Rosmarinus officinalis* 'Miss Jessop's Variety'
2 *Lavandula augustifolia* 'Vera'
1 *Rhododendron* 'Pink Pearl'
2 *Aucuba japonica* 'Longifolia'
1 *Viburnum rhytidophyllum*
2 *Garrya elliptica*
3 *Hypericum patulum* 'Hidcote'
2 *Philadelphus* 'Belle Etoile'
3 *Ribes sanguineum* 'Pulborough Scarlet'
1 *Yucca flaccida*
3 *Rosmarinus officinalis* 'Miss Jessop's Variety'

3 *Potentilla fruticosa* 'Yellow Queen'
3 *Mahonia bealii*
3 *Senecio greyi*
4 *Bergenia delavayi*
1 *Choisya ternata*
2 *Berberis thunbergii*
5 *Hosta sieboldiana*
3 *Cytisus* × *kewensis*
3 *Mahonia* 'Charity'
3 *Potentilla fruticosa* 'Yellow Queen'
3 *Potentilla fruticosa* 'Katherine Dykes'
3 *Iris delavayi*

ANNUALS
HERBS

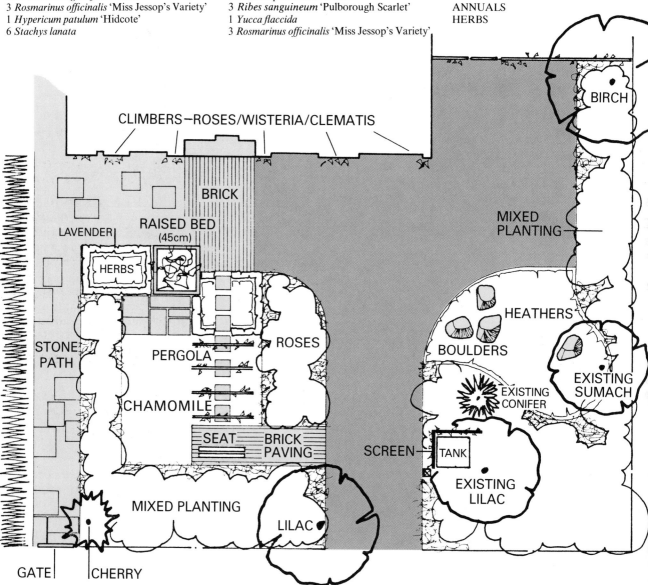

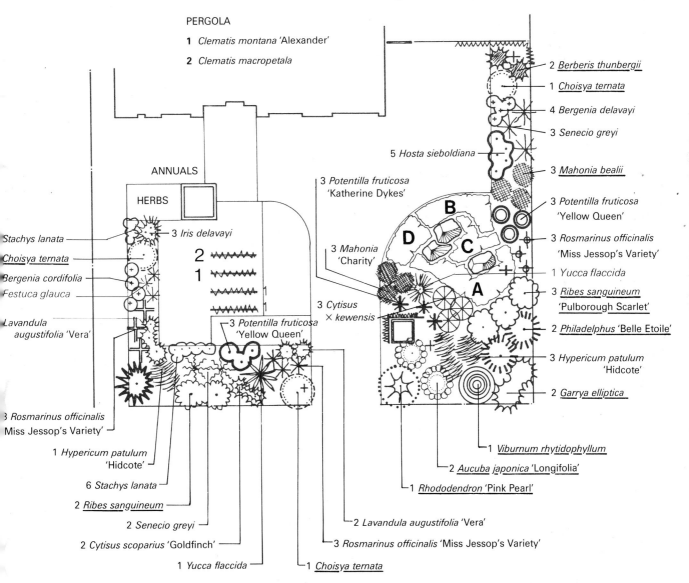

A *Erica carnea* 'Myretoun Ruby'

B *Erica carnea* 'Purple Beauty'

C *Erica carnea* 'Springwood White'

D *Calluna vulgaris* 'Robert Chapman'

PERGOLA

1 *Clematis montana* 'Alexander'

2 *Clematis macropetala*

2 <u>*Berberis thunbergii*</u>

1 <u>*Choisya ternata*</u>

4 *Bergenia delavayi*

3 *Senecio greyi*

5 *Hosta sieboldiana*

3 <u>*Mahonia bealii*</u>

3 *Potentilla fruticosa* 'Katherine Dykes'

3 *Potentilla fruticosa* 'Yellow Queen'

3 *Rosmarinus officinalis* 'Miss Jessop's Variety'

ANNUALS

HERBS

3 *Mahonia* 'Charity'

1 *Yucca flaccida*

3 <u>*Ribes sanguineum*</u> 'Pulborough Scarlet'

Stachys lanata

<u>Choisya ternata</u>

Bergenia cordifolia

Festuca glauca

3 *Iris delavayi*

3 *Cytisus* × *kewensis*

2 <u>*Philadelphus* 'Belle Etoile'</u>

3 *Hypericum patulum* 'Hidcote'

Lavandula augustifolia 'Vera'

3 *Potentilla fruticosa* 'Yellow Queen'

2 <u>*Garrya elliptica*</u>

3 *Rosmarinus officinalis* Miss Jessop's Variety'

1 *Hypericum patulum* 'Hidcote'

6 *Stachys lanata*

2 <u>*Ribes sanguineum*</u>

2 *Senecio greyi*

2 *Cytisus scoparius* 'Goldfinch'

1 *Yucca flaccida*

1 <u>*Viburnum rhytidophyllum*</u>

2 <u>*Aucuba japonica* 'Longifolia'</u>

1 <u>*Rhododendron* 'Pink Pearl'</u>

2 *Lavandula augustifolia* 'Vera'

3 *Rosmarinus officinalis* 'Miss Jessop's Variety'

1 <u>*Choisya ternata*</u>

Figure 7.3 In this small rectangular garden the planting reinforces the strong flowing curves of the ground plan. Notice how material is used in groups, even in this limited area. The framework plants are underlined.

PLANTING LIST

2 *Fatsia japonica*
1 *Pyracantha rogersiana* (on fence)
2 *Hydrangea macrophylla* 'Blue Wave'
1 *Robinia pseudoacacia* 'Frisia'
2 *Arundinaria nitida*
1 *Ribes sanguineum*
1 *Jasminum nudiflorum* (against fence)
1 *Spirea × bumalda* 'Anthony Waterer'
1 *Clematis macropetala* (on fence)
1 *Weigela florida* 'Variegata'
2 *Cistus cyprius*

1 Climbing rose 'Danse de Feu' (on fence)
3 *Hebe subalpina*
1 *Choisya ternata*
1 *Jasminum officinale*
1 *Wisteria sinensis*
4 *Hosta sieboldiana*
1 *Helleborus corsicus*
1 *Rosmarinus officinalis*
2 *Salvia officinalis* 'Purpurea'
1 *Hebe* 'Midsummer Beauty'
1 *Lonicera japonica* 'Halliana' (on fence)
1 *Acanthus mollis*
5 *Euphorbia polychroma*

1 *Yucca flaccida*
1 *Vitis coignetiae* (on fence)
2 *Cytisus scoparius* 'Goldfinch'
1 *Betula pendula*
1 *Buddleia davidii* 'Empire Blue'
1 *Miscanthus sinensis*
1 *Philadelphus* 'Belle Etoile'
1 *Hedera colchica* 'Paddy's Pride' (on fence)
2 *Elaeagnus pungens* 'Maculata'
1 *Mahonia lomariifolia*
4 *Potentilla fruticosa* 'Red Ace'
3 Cream lupins
6 H.T. Bush roses
2 *Phlomis fruticosa*
3 *Festuca glauca*
1 *Euphorbia griffithii* 'Fireglow'

ANNUALS

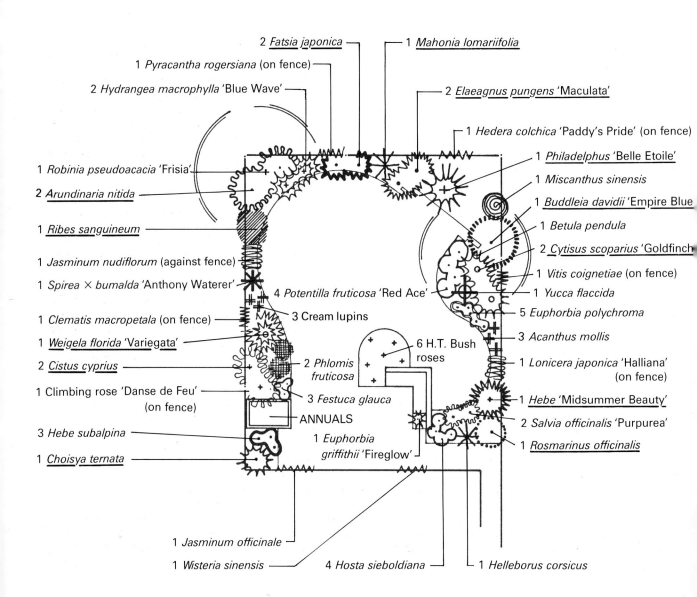

Figure 7.4 The variety of tree shapes is considerable and each will have a direct influence on the design of your garden.

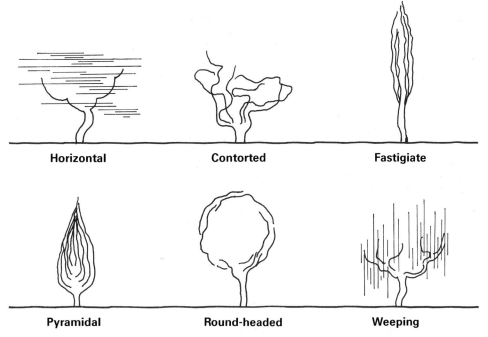

Horizontal

Contorted

Fastigiate

Pyramidal

Round-headed

Weeping

with sweetly scented winter flowers; cherry laurel *Prunus laurocerasus*; bamboos that include *Arundinaria nitida*, *A. murielae* and *A. japonica* are but a few of the sturdy types of plants you may need. Many of these are nicknamed 'architectural plants' because they rely on their overall shape and texture of foliage rather than an instant garish display of colour. In many ways this is what you want as a restful backdrop helps to provide a feeling of calm and stability in a garden.

Not all background planting need be evergreen; berberis, weigela, *Kerria japonica*, *Ribes sanguineum*, corylus and philadelphus are excellent large deciduous shrubs worth consideration.

Trees

Within the framework you must also consider trees. You worked out the positions of these in the general design of your garden, where their vertical emphasis played an important role in the overall composition, but you now need to work out which shapes (see Figure 7.4) and sizes are right for your garden.

SHAPES AND SIZES. The shape and eventual size of trees varies greatly and the folly of planting a weeping willow in a confined space, usually a front garden, is soon obvious as the plant quickly outstrips its surrounds, blocks out light and dwarfs the building. The insensitive remedy of hacking back branches should never be encouraged as it simply mutilates any tree and prevents it reaching its natural proportions. The correct setting for a weeping willow is by water, and preferably a large sheet of water. This is not simply because it likes moist conditions but because of the marvellous visual contrast made by the strong vertical line of stems and foliage with the horizontal plane beneath it.

As a general rule, do not plant rampant species such as poplar or willow close to buildings, particularly if the ground is shrinkable clay. These trees can cause serious problems to foundations. You do see mature forest trees such as oak, hornbeam and plane extremely close to freestanding walls and houses with little or no obvious damage, but a safe guideline is never to plant a tree closer to a structure than its eventual height.

The sizes of trees range from Lombardy poplars and tall conifers on the largest scale to the Japanese cherry 'Amanogawa' lower down, while miniature conifers echo the line at ground level. All these need careful handling as too many focal points produce a busy, restless composition.

In the final analysis the size of trees needs to reflect the scale of your garden. Forest trees balance out a parkland setting. Small ornamental trees do exactly the same in an intimate suburban setting. The rules that crop up in all parts of this book are sympathy and simplicity, and they relate to soft landscape just as much as to any other area of the design exercise.

Fastigiate trees (those with a conical or tapering outline), with their soaring branches, look and act as punctuation marks in the garden, drawing the eye in a particular direction. Other shapes include the rather odd, contorted or twisted trees, mop-headed, flat-topped and horizontal. Most of our indigenous varieties, such as ash, oak, birch and wild cherry, are roughly circular or oval and to be honest these generally look most comfortable in Britain's temperate climate.

EVERGREEN AND DECIDUOUS TREES. Bear in mind the obvious difference between evergreen and deciduous trees. Not all conifers are evergreen, however, larch being a good example. Neither are all oaks deciduous: *Quercus ilex* is an evergreen oak. In other words, check the species and variety to build up an accurate picture. Foliage may be dense or light, casting shadow accordingly and affecting the ground below, for example birch and eucalyptus trees cast little shade, sycamore and lime cast a great deal. The latter also excretes sticky drops that make car-cleaning a nightmare, so never plant limes beside a drive.

FLOWERING TREES provide a bonus in the late winter, spring and early summer. Some of the garish pink cherries can be a little overpowering, however, and a worthwhile foil is our native *Prunus avium* or gean, with a wealth of white blossom. Fruit can be decorative, too, as in the flowering crab apples (*Malus*), rowans (*Sorbus*), or the Indian bean tree (*Catalpa*) with great green clusters of what look like french beans. Edible fruits include the apples, pears, plums, peaches and many other species, all of which have the benefit of blossom early in the year.

TREE-PLANTING. Before leaving the subject of trees I will consider planting. While most of us prepare the ground for shrubs and herbaceous material with loving care, trees somehow seem to get left out, being dropped into any old hole and supported with a bamboo cane.

• Always prepare a hole of ample size to accept the tree roots when spread out. Break up the bottom and sides

with a fork and drive a stout stake into the ground at this stage rather than risking a shattered root when the tree is in position. Mix peat or well-rotted leaf-mould into the removed soil. Place the tree in the hole, bearing in mind that the new soil level should match the level of the soil when the tree was lifted. Backfill soil a layer at a time, firming the ground as you go. Finally, attach the tree to the stake with two plastic ties. Never use wire, old tights or string, because they will either fail or cut the tree in half after a couple of years. Mulch the ground around the tree with a 5 cm thick layer of well-rotted organic matter.

Hedges (see Figure 7.5)

Hedges are halfway between trees and shrubs in visual terms. They can form the boundaries of a garden or they can act as internal screens. They work out a lot cheaper than walls or fences and a mature hedge provides virtually as much shelter and security as either of these.

Maintenance is a factor to be reckoned with and the overuse of privet, with its endless need for clipping and its greedy roots, does nothing to further the cause. Yew, beech and hornbeam on the other hand need a once-yearly trim, grow to virtually any height and provide

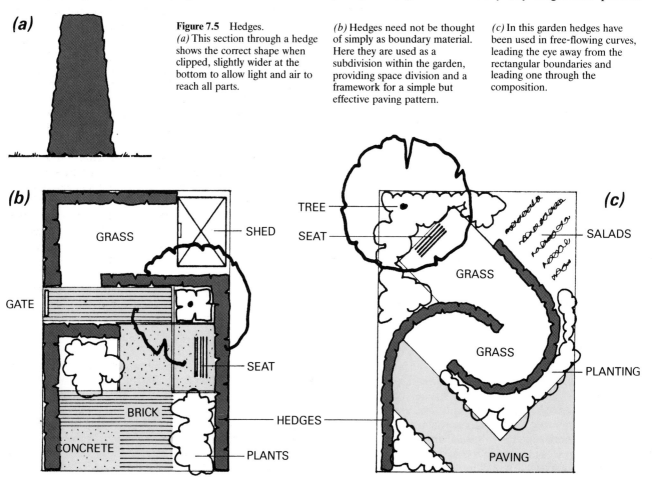

Figure 7.5 Hedges.
(a) This section through a hedge shows the correct shape when clipped, slightly wider at the bottom to allow light and air to reach all parts.

(b) Hedges need not be thought of as simply as boundary material. Here they are used as a subdivision within the garden, providing space division and a framework for a simple but effective paving pattern.

(c) In this garden hedges have been used in free-flowing curves, leading the eye away from the rectangular boundaries and leading one through the composition.

interest throughout the year. Yew is evergreen, while beech and hornbeam hold some of their dried-up leaves throughout the winter.

Of course, not all hedges need clipping to a rigid shape: many shrubs simply planted in a line create an informal boundary, although this will inevitably be quite wide. Escallonia, *Rosa rugosa*, berberis (with its deterrent spines), choisya and, of course, laurel all produce loose hedges of differing characters.

In a rural setting a field hedge of hawthorn and blackthorn is totally stock-proof and, although elm trees are a thing of the past, elm suckers still form a high proportion of many field hedges. Depending on the part of the country in which you live you may also find wild viburnum, hazel, elder and field maple.

In these three differing styles of hedge there is a transition from formality, through informality – in both cases using garden plants – to an indigenous hedge of wild species that has a rural feel.

There is much complaint that hedges take too long to grow, and there is some truth in this, but it is possible to erect a temporary fence of, say, wattle hurdles while the hedge develops. To give your hedge a good start it is essential to prepare a well-manured and well-dug trench prior to planting. And like all other plants, hedges benefit from regular feeding, which will be reflected in increased vigour and earlier maturity.

Most of those shrubs just mentioned grow to a reasonable height and are for use primarily as a boundary. Within the garden, however, you can use much lower hedges to act as a frame for specialised planting, to form a geometric pattern, or to provide particular space division without blocking out a view entirely. Clipped lavender and box spring to mind immediately. Both are ideal for edging a knot garden for herbs or forming the outline of a formal rose garden. Both are evergreen and lavender – the best variety is 'Hidcote' – has the added bonus of deliciously fragrant flowers that can be cut and used for lavender bags.

Lonicera nitida is another small-leaved evergreen, often confused with box but in fact a member of the honeysuckle family. It forms a neat little hedge, if regularly clipped, but keep it below 60 cm if possible as it has a tendency to become straggly.

I have left conifers to last. There is no doubt that they form fast-growing and dense hedges, but in a domestic situation they tend to be overused and grow to form enormous funeral backcloths that dominate rather than add to a design.

Filling in

Now that you have completed the framework of your planting plan you can begin to select the lighter, more colourful material which will fill it in. The plants most suitable for this 'filling in' stage are smaller shrubs and herbaceous plants, some ground-covering plants, bulbs and annuals. But before choosing these, consider how you will use colour in your composition.

Use of colour

That great Victorian/Edwardian plantswoman Gertrude Jekyll worked with the architect Sir Edwin Lutyens and this combination produced some of the finest houses and gardens built at the turn of the century. Although Gertrude Jekyll's gardens were mostly on a far grander scale than is normal today, her philosophy of planting design remains faultless.

This revolved largely around the way in which she used colour, both in ranges and intensity, and reflected her not inconsiderable talent as a painter who greatly admired the impressionist school. She suggested that in broad terms hot colours such as red, yellow and orange should be in one category while the cooler blues, pinks, purples and mauves should be in another. Hot colours are vibrant and, if used some way from a viewpoint, have the effect of drawing the eye and foreshortening the distance. This is easily demonstrated if a bed of bright red salvias is placed at the bottom of a long, narrow garden: instead of there being a restful view that could encompass several focal points and a rhythmic pattern, the eye is instantly riveted and everything else becomes subsidiary to this one dominant feature. The solution to this is to site the hot colours close to the house or main viewpoint and the softer cooler colours further away. Grey, as in most design work, is a great harmoniser, toning and linking ranges together. A particularly telling and successful combination is purple and grey. *Berberis thunbergii* 'Atropurpurea' planted alongside *Senecio greyi*, or *Phlomis fruticosa* with *Sedum spectabile* 'Autumn Joy' are excellent examples of this.

Taken to extremes you can work entirely in a single colour as the superb White Garden at Sissinghurst demonstrates. Such a treatment, although dazzling in its simplicity, needs a positive contrast elsewhere and the great joy of Sissinghurst is the movement from one garden room to another, each having a quite different theme.

In a domestic situation you can treat annual bedding schemes or roses in a similar way. Roses *en bloc* in a single colour form a very positive statement, while mixed roses in a colour range are also effective. Mixing roses out of separate hot and cool ranges is, however, asking for trouble and seldom works.

Shrubs and herbaceous plants

While in general you should keep to the colour ranges which I have just described, there is no harm in introducing an accent of colour out of context. The singing red flowers of *Geum borisii*, for instance, will form a dramatic pinpoint against a predominantly cool border, while the lime green bracts of *Euphorbia polychroma* make the great red leaves of *Rheum palmatum rubrum* even more dramatic. It is this sort of flair and originality that brings a border to life.

The shape of a plant is yet another factor to be considered: for example, you could use upright against rounded, as a group of yuccas in front of broom or hebe. The same effect will be gained by planting that marvellous architectural spurge *Euphorbia wulfenii* in conjunction with the fastigiate Irish yew, *Taxus baccata* 'Fastigiata'.

It is fair to say that the true herbaceous border is largely a thing of the past. The labour in digging, staking, tying and dividing consumes more than its fair share of time in this day and age. Conversely, a border comprised entirely of shrubs becomes visually heavy, as you can see in many of our municipal parks. Combining the two, however, has enormous advantages; the shrubs provide shelter and support for the perennial material, which helps to bring colour and added interest.

If you do want a herbaceous border it makes sense to site it where it is not in constant view, as it will appear devoid of life during the long winter months. The general rules of planting design still apply, however, as far as colours, shape and texture are concerned.

Ground cover

I have already discussed the use of large areas of ground cover, but the use of ground cover is equally pertinent under both deciduous and evergreen shrubs, to help eliminate weed growth. The most effective varieties are evergreen and the choice is wide. Some, such as *Hypericum calycinum* and *Lamium galeobdolon*, are rampant and useful only where they can be allowed free rein to romp about endlessly. Others are less invasive and many, such as epimedium, geranium and pulmonaria, have the added attraction of flowers. By using ground cover you can create great drifts of foliage, linking several of the overhead species together. This is of enormous importance, providing continuity as well as retaining moisture in the form of a living mulch.

Bulbs

Bulbs can be used in two ways, either as serried ranks of annual colour, which tend to smack of the local park, or naturalised in borders or rougher grass when they really become a sort of instant ground cover. The formal approach can be effective in an architectural setting close to a building, particularly if the house is classical. In this case it is best to stick to blocks of colour and varieties. Some dramatic combinations can be set up: pale blue or white polyanthus or violas are superb under deep blue hyacinths, while pink tulips over aubrieta can be stunning.

A less formal approach, with a lot less work, involves naturalisation. This can be particularly useful in a young border where there are gaps between shrubs or herbaceous planting. A sweep of trumpet daffodils or groups of rather more delicate species of narcissus in a bed both

look charming. They do, of course, produce masses of leaves which must be left to die down naturally. This means that they are not suitable in a lawn but are just right for rougher grass that need not be cut until early June.

Annual bedding

The approach for annuals is really the same as for bulbs, using a formal or informal treatment. The only difference is the fact that they will need discarding as soon as frost sets in. Take the approach mentioned in Chapter 6: instead of undertaking the laborious job of growing from seed in the greenhouse, pricking out and finally planting, it can make sense simply to hand-sow drifts and thin them out as they come through. The cost is negligible when compared to plants bought in boxes, and the results are often superb. Don't forget the huge and grandiose sunflowers to fill the back of a bed or the incomparable evening fragrance of a bed of nicotiana close to french windows.

For more help with choosing plants see Philip Swindells, *The Flower Garden*, another book in this series.

Your planting plan is complete, but before you buy your plants you must prepare your ground to receive them.

GROUND PREPARATION

Soil

You have already looked at your soil type and structure and this will determine the way in which you handle the cultivation of your soil.

If you live on a new development your soil may have been over-compacted by site traffic, buried underneath a layer of subsoil or even carted away altogether. In the last case you will have to bring in topsoil. If you do this, try to find out its source: it is not unknown for poor-quality soil and even subsoil to be sold as good topsoil. Colour and feel are often fair indicators: topsoil is usually dark and friable. Also make sure that you bring in enough soil for the job. Remember that different types of plant require different depths of soil. Grass for a good lawn should have about 7.5 cm of topsoil with adequate drainage, most shrubs and herbaceous material will thrive in 23–30 cm while trees require at least 45 cm. The latter can, of course, be positioned in specially dug pits, but in general terms the deeper the layer of topsoil, the better any plant will grow.

If your garden has been worked for years, the quality of your soil may have deteriorated. Plants take nourishment from the ground and if nothing is replaced the soil becomes steadily poorer and in the end is able to support very little. You can improve it by adding fertiliser as you dig.

Fertiliser comes in two basic types, organic and inorganic. While the first is entirely natural in its origins, the latter is factory-produced. Both can contain the three basic growing elements, nitrogen, phosphorus and potassium, as well as other trace elements, but organic fertilisers encourage beneficial soil bacteria, while inorganic types (though often faster-acting) do not.

The great benefit of bulky organic fertiliser is that it is also a soil conditioner (see Chapter 1, 'Basic assessments'). In addition it is far cheaper than inorganic materials, especially if you have a worthwhile compost heap or access to stables or a farm. Inorganically fed ground can remain either heavy or light and in the latter case soil erosion by wind can be a real problem.

Waterlogging excludes oxygen and if this is a serious problem then a drainage system of one kind or another will be necessary (see Chapter 3, 'Levels and drainage').

Cultivation

Once you have established a suitable depth of topsoil and adequate drainage you must cultivate your soil thoroughly. Single-digging of one spit or spade's depth is normally sufficient but if you are breaking new ground or growing vegetables, then double-digging to two spades' depth may be in order. When you carry out the latter, be sure not to mix topsoil and subsoil. Simply turn the ground over at the lower level, incorporating manure as you do so.

Hand cultivation is inevitably slow and also hard work, so tackle it over a reasonable period of time. On the positive side it is the surest way to remove perennial weeds, including the pernicious ground elder and convolvulus. You can also root out all the buried rubbish left behind by builders.

You could use a rotary cultivator instead. However, some of these are worse than useless, bouncing about on the surface, chopping weed roots into a thousand small and vigorous pieces and simply compacting the ground below. A good rotary cultivator digs deep and thoroughly, but it is worth bearing in mind that it will not kill weeds and it will leave the soil very soft and fluffy. Use a rotavator as a means of quickly cultivating clean soil on ground that has already been cleared of weeds and their roots, but do not rotavate the same patch of ground year after year.

CHECKPOINT

Now that you have read this chapter you should have chosen the plants which will be most successful in your location, having taken into account the effects of your microclimate, and used your knowledge of planting design to form a pattern which will provide colour and interest all the year as well as fitting into the scale of your garden. You should also be able to prepare your ground to receive your plants.

To check that you have understood the points made in this chapter, answer the following questions.

1 Which three factors affect your choice of plants for your garden?
2 If you lived in an area subject to high winds which two species of shrub could you plant to provide shelter and what effect would they have on the movement of air?
3 Which two fast-growing species could you grow in your garden to give interest while you are waiting for your long-term species to fill out?
4 Why is it important always to use the correct botanical names for plants when you buy them and when you refer to them?
5 What types of plant would you use as a framework for the lighter, more colourful material in your garden?
6 Which trees act as punctuation marks in a garden?
7 What factor should influence the size of the trees you choose for your garden?
8 Which three shrubs could you use to create an informal hedge?
9 How can you avoid 'visual chaos' in a small garden?
10 What should be the condition of your soil before you put in your plants and how can you achieve this?

Check your answers against the information given in the chapter.

CHAPTER EIGHT

Features
and
furnishings

*Ornamental pools/Other water features/Swimming pools
Paddling pools/Rock gardens and rock features
Barbecues/Seats/Pergolas/Overhead beams/Arbours
Summer-houses and conservatories/Gazebos
Play areas/Lighting and power/Furnishings
Checkpoint*

Now that you have designed your planting, you have, in basic terms, rounded off your overall garden plan, but there still remain other components to fit into the composition. These are features which you included in your original list in Chapter 1, such as pools, both ornamental and swimming, rockeries, barbecues, pergolas, summer-houses, sandpit and play areas. You have already roughed in the positions for these but to finalise them you need to understand the relationship between these features and other parts of the garden. Also you need to know how they should be constructed.

Obviously, you will not have included all the above features in your design and consequently you may not wish to read every section of this chapter. To enable you to find easily the sections you need, Table 8.1 lists the features I shall discuss and the page numbers on which you can find them.

Table 8.1 **Additional garden features and furnishings**

ORNAMENTAL POOLS

Water can be delightful in a garden, and very often it is the sound of it that is refreshing on a hot summer's day. You need not have a vast lake or Geneva-type fountain for water to be effective; a small pool with a bubble jet is just as enjoyable. Remember that prime rule of simplicity. In addition, oversized fountains in a small area

of water quickly lead to problems, particularly if a breeze is blowing, because the pool is very soon emptied!

Where should I site my pool?
Unfortunately, many pools are sited with little thought. An open situation is really essential as neither aquatic plants nor fish thrive in total shade and the latter certainly dislike the pollution caused by leaves and other vegetation that can fall into the water.

What is the best shape for a pool?
The shape of your pool depends on its location within your garden and this in broad terms relates to its distance from the house. If your pool is close to a building or sitting area then an architectural shape will be suitable, linking and blending with the lines of paving and walling round about. If your pool is in a more distant part of your garden it can be less formal, possibly echoing the strong, flowing curves of lawns and borders.

Remember, too, that shapes on the drawing board look very different on the ground and what may look like an intriguing design might be a mess in reality – another good reason for keeping things simple.

How big should my pool be?
The success of a pool relies on a balanced ecology of fish, insect and plant life so it is obvious that, within reason, the larger your pool the better. It is very difficult to achieve a balance in a small pool and as a guide you will encounter problems with anything less than about 2 m square.

How deep should I make it?
From above ground you simply see the outline of a pool, but its shape and depth below water level – the profile as it is called – are also vitally important. Contrary to common belief, a garden pool need be no more than 45 cm deep as most deep-water plants and fish thrive at this depth. Many plants, however, enjoy just having their 'feet' in the water and for these a 'marginal' shelf should be constructed around approximately two-thirds of the circumference. This should be about 23 cm below the surface and about 30 cm wide. If this shelf is built in two sections bays will be left around the perimeter which form ideal breeding areas for fish.

Could I have more than one pool?

If your garden slopes naturally or you have created different levels by 'cut and fill', you may wish to incorporate a number of pools, one falling to another, or connected by some sort of stream. Such an arrangement can, again, be formal or informal but any such composition should be carefully thought out if it is not to look contrived. If you are lucky enough to have a stream in the garden this will ensure a non-stop supply of fresh water, but you will have to fit grids to retain any fish. In a normal situation water will need to be recirculated, and submersible pumps of various capacities are available to carry this out.

Making an ornamental pool

Traditionally, garden pools were always made from concrete, but problems were inevitable with ground movement and frost inducing hair-line cracks that were almost impossible to find. Construction was difficult and time-consuming, and this was reflected in relatively high costs. Over the last 20 years or so various sheet rubbers and plastics, commonly called 'liners', have revolutionised pool construction. Such liners are easy to install and can fit complex shapes that would have been virtually impossible in concrete. As well as flexible liners, moulded pools are also available.

Pool liners

POLYTHENE. This is the cheapest type of pool liner. It can be very tempting to use builders' polythene, straight off the roll, and in fact many people do so. It is, however, extremely fragile, does not stretch and is impossible to patch if holed. It is quite simply false economy to use this material and you could lose a valuable collection of plants and fish in consequence.

LAMINATED PVC. This looks much the same as polythene but is far tougher as it is usually made up of a sandwich of three sheets. It can be stretched to conform to the shape of a pool and has a life expectancy of at least 20 years. For most domestic purposes it is ideal.

BUTYL RUBBER. This is extremely tough and is used commercially for lining reservoirs. In the garden it is ideal for large ponds or lakes but the disadvantage is that it is expensive.

What do I need to construct a liner pool?

You will need the following equipment and materials: a spade, shovel, pickaxe, plywood template angled at 20°, long straight edge, spirit level, soft sand, and a pool liner. Many shops and garden centres sell liners of a specific size to fit a pre-calculated depth and surface area. If you want to work out your own specifications, simply add twice the maximum depth of the pool to the maximum width and length and this will give you a sheet of ample size.

As far as the colour of the liner is concerned, steer clear of sky blue and in particular avoid the simulated pebble beach finish. Black is best, as this increases surface reflection and makes the bottom virtually invisible.

Before you start work, remember that the edge or coping of the pool must be absolutely level; if it is not you will end up with the water looking as if it is standing at an angle. If your garden slopes at the point you wish to set the pool either the surrounding lawn or planting will have to sweep down around the water, or, in a formal situation, a retaining wall will be necessary on the lower sides to keep the coping horizontal.

● The construction of a liner pool is shown in Figure 8.1. For a free-form pool in, say, a lawn area, first mark out the entire area of the pool and coping. Use a line swung from a cane set in the centre of the circles involved to work out the curves and carefully lift the turf with a sharp spade, stacking it for use elsewhere in the garden. Next mark out the shape of the pool and dig out all the ground within this line to a depth of 23 cm, angling in the sides of the excavation to approximately 20°. As the soil you dig out will almost certainly be fertile topsoil, stack this also for re-use; it could be particularly useful for filling a raised bed in another part of your design. This operation has taken you to the depth of the marginal shelf. When you have marked the extent of this shelf, excavate the rest of the pool to the finished depth.

Remove any sharp stones from the bottom and sides and then trowel a layer of damp, soft sand on to the bottom and sides using a steel float (a rectangular trowel).

Now place the liner over the excavation and weight it down at the edges with loosely laid coping stones. Fill the pool and trim down the surrounding plastic to leave a flap of about 30 cm all round. As the pool is a free-form shape there will be wrinkles around the edge. Slit these so that the liner lies flat and lay the coping on a mortar mix so that it overhangs the edge by 5 cm. This last detail is important, as the slabs, or whatever material you use, cast a shadow over the water, softening the harder line of the coping.

Moulded pools

FIBREGLASS POOLS. These are pre-formed to a number of patterns and you can simply bed them on sand in suitable excavations. Their drawback lies mainly in their size – most are not large enough to support a balanced environment – and in addition they are expensive.

VACUUM-FORMED PVC POOLS. Vacuum-formed PVC pools look much the same as fibreglass ones but are thinner and far more brittle. They are cheaper but have a short life expectancy, particularly if boisterous children are present!

Stocking and maintaining your pool

I have already said that a pool needs a balance of plant, fish and insect life, and many garden centres now sell complete collections that take the guesswork out of stocking a pool. Their contents are worked out according to the surface area of water involved. Do not be too concerned if after you have stocked a new pool it goes green. This is simply due to an explosion of algal growth and clears once aquatic plants and fish form a natural balance, usually after about three to six months.

Another fallacy is that a pool should be drained and cleaned out on a regular basis. This should never be done as it completely upsets the cycle so carefully built up. In a small pool, simply remove about a quarter of the water and replace it with fresh once a year. This prevents the undue build-up of toxins. If leaves are a problem spread a plastic net over the pool as autumn draws on and

Figure 8.1 Fitting a pool liner.

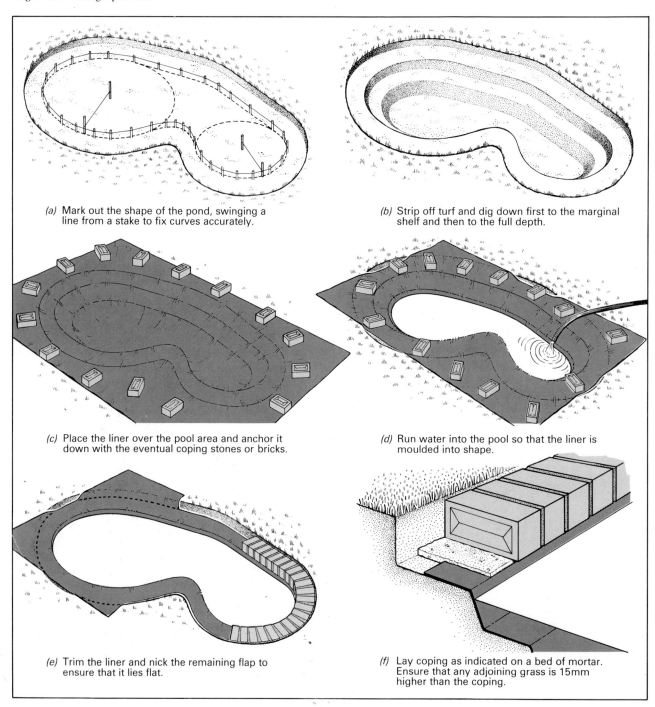

(a) Mark out the shape of the pond, swinging a line from a stake to fix curves accurately.

(b) Strip off turf and dig down first to the marginal shelf and then to the full depth.

(c) Place the liner over the pool area and anchor it down with the eventual coping stones or bricks.

(d) Run water into the pool so that the liner is moulded into shape.

(e) Trim the liner and nick the remaining flap to ensure that it lies flat.

(f) Lay coping as indicated on a bed of mortar. Ensure that any adjoining grass is 15mm higher than the coping.

remove both it and the leaves once the leaves have all fallen. Top up the pool in summer to keep pace with evaporation.

Pumps

Contrary to common belief, moving water is not essential for healthy pond life, but a simple fountain, cascade or stream can provide enormous interest. The old rule was that to move large volumes you had to use a surface pump and this involved complicated plumbing and chambers. Today, however, submersible pumps can handle enormous flows and they can be neatly installed on the bottom of a pool with an outlet pipe to a fountain, waterfall or both by means of a junction piece.

OTHER WATER FEATURES

If you have young children you may feel that an ornamental pool could be a danger, but this does not mean that it is impossible for you to have a water feature in the garden.

You can use a millstone or solid piece of slate set over a water tank sunk into the ground. Piers support the stone, a submersible pump fits in the bottom of the tank and a pipe allows water to be pushed up through a central hole to bubble and slide over the surface. This sort of feature is ideal in a garden where a conventional pool would be a danger to very young children.

Otherwise, why not start off with a raised bed or sandpit about 45 cm above the ground and convert it to an ornamental pool when your children are older (see Figure 8.2)? As it is raised, you could cover it on occasions to double as a seat. This makes an attractive feature in any garden.

Figure 8.2 This water feature has been built within a raised bed and consists of a slate or stone slab set on two brick piers within a plastic water tank. A submersible pump recycles the water. The area around the piers is filled with smooth stones and cobbles.

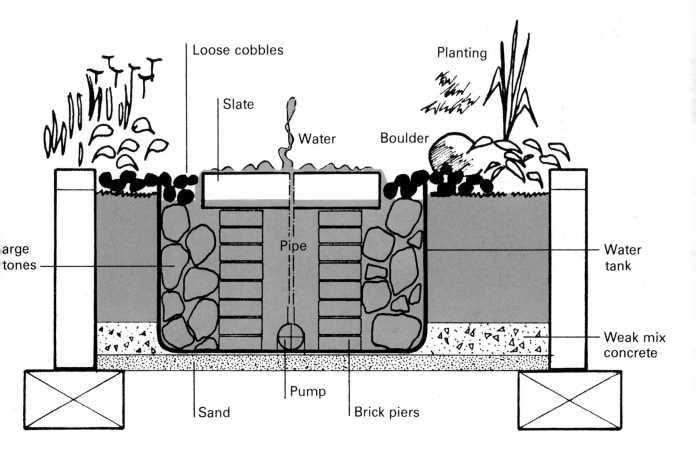

SWIMMING POOLS

Swimming pools are large, dominating features and while they can look most inviting during those hot summer months, they can seem correspondingly bleak in the winter. In consequence they need careful siting: you might not want a pool so close to the house that you can see it all the time, but it is obviously important to site it in a sunny position.

How should it fit into my garden design?

If you decide to keep a pool close to the house all the rules of hard landscape apply. It should link positively into a paving pattern that in turn fits into the overall composition of house and garden. Close to a building an architectural shape – rectangular or at least geometric – will make sense. The ubiquitous kidney shape is visually feeble; there are far better free-flowing designs that can be worked out simply using pencil, ruler and a pair of compasses. Do not be talked into a specific shape by a pool supplier – nearly any shape is possible, particularly when you are spending a good deal of money.

What are swimming pools made from?

Constructional methods vary from patent concrete interlocking blocks that are laid, rendered and tiled, and concrete that is sprayed under pressure from a hose, to pool liners. All of these have an excellent life expectancy if installed properly.

Could I construct my own pool?

It is possible to construct your own pool, employing a mechanical digger and then installing the shell in kit form, bought from a supplier. In many ways, however, this is a false economy. In my opinion pool construction is a job for experts. In addition to this, a reputable company will offer a guarantee that can be worth its weight in gold. Bear in mind that pump equipment will need housing and a changing room is often helpful. Usually both these functions can be catered for under one roof and a small building or summer-house can be incorporated within the design.

There are available certain above-ground pools, in a frightful shade of blue. Although these are cheaper, they are visually unpleasant and unless screened completely are best left out of any design scheme.

PADDLING POOLS

These are altogether different from swimming pools and are essential for toddlers, who adore water. They can be bought off the peg and the rigid PVC or fibreglass varieties are better than the flimsy plastic sort that sit inside an assembled frame. Alternatively, why not construct a simple water splash on or near a terrace area? This could consist of a depression in the surrounding paving with a brushed aggregate finish to prevent slipping. It could either be simply filled with water or have an over-

head shower which will make for hours of enjoyment. Such a feature could link very sensibly into an overall paving pattern.

ROCK GARDENS AND ROCK FEATURES

Rocks for a rock garden

The whole question of rock gardens, rockeries and rock features is a complex one. So often you see what can only be described as the 'currant bun' rockery: pieces of stone, or at worst concrete, set at random in a mound of soil to produce a most unhappy, and far from natural, end result.

It is this word 'natural' that really sums it all up. A rockery should be just so, echoing a situation found in the landscape. To use Westmorland stone in Surrey or Forest of Dean rock in East Anglia makes a mockery of the idea. Not only do such stones look completely out of character, but they cost a fortune in transport charges, something that is capitalised upon by hauliers and garden centres alike. Most areas have their own local stone, whether it be granite, slate, sandstone or limestone. The fact of the matter is that many of these are not thought to be fashionable, which is total nonsense. They can all make first-class outcrops. What is needed is a sympathetic understanding of the material.

This brings me on to the method in which the rock is set; it certainly should not be dumped simply any old how. Most stones, certainly the sedimentary type rocks, were laid down in layers, either horizontally or more often at a slight angle, and you can see these naturally as outcrops. Such an alignment is called a 'bedding plane' in geological terms and you should copy this when you build a rockery in your garden. This means setting the rocks along a bedding plane of your own choosing.

The larger the pieces of rock you use the better. Obviously, this will be limited by the labour available. If you have the room and the money to use a mechanical digger, do so. It will carry out the work in a short time and produce a spectacular end result. Since most outcrops are seen in a sloping situation, rock will look comfortable if your garden slopes. If the site is flat, then you will be involved in major earth moving to create anything like a convincing outcrop. In this case it may be sensible to forget rock and think of something else as a feature!

Planting for a rock garden

Planting for a rock garden should also be as natural as possible and here you can create conditions that are out of the question elsewhere in the garden. You can fill sharply draining pockets with small stones to provide a host for alpine plants demanding sharp drainage, while many of the smaller coniferous trees will thrive here, forming a collection which looks so much better than planting them at random in other parts of the garden where they might provide too many 'punctuation marks'.

Other rock features

It seems a shame that after spending what may be a considerable sum on rock, you should then cover most of it up, as again you very often see only the face in a natural setting.

But you can use rock in an entirely different way. You can form bold sculptures of one or two carefully positioned pieces in much the same way as in Japanese gardens. The latter have religious and social significance but you can certainly use this sculptural approach to good advantage. The point to remember is that your composition should be one thing or the other, either totally natural or stunningly dramatic. The grey areas in between are a disaster.

Occasionally an outcrop of rock can look superb in a terrace, patio or strongly architectural area, but it will need impeccable handling. More often such a feature will blend in to the more informal part of a garden, preferably in a position that catches plenty of sun.

BARBECUES

Barbecues are becoming increasingly popular. If you are hooked on the hobby – and many people are – a built-in barbecue may be far more practical, and is certainly neater, than the shop-bought rickety variety, balanced on spindly legs. A barbecue with a built-in seat and adjoining wall can form the focus of a sitting area (see Figure 8.3). It might be constructed of bricks to link with the house and paving, and can be built big enough to feed an ample gathering of friends – something that not many off-the-peg barbecues can do! Nor need a barbecue area necessarily be close to the house, although proximity to a kitchen is useful; it might be sited with a swimming pool or in a part of the garden that catches the evening sun.

Figure 8.3 A barbecue. The plan and elevation show basic constructional techniques. The cooking and charcoal grids can be moved up and down, and the store cupboard is useful for tools. A built-in seat and the wall behind make this a focus of any outdoor living area.

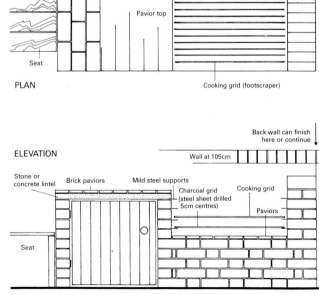

SEATS

Most seats are really furnishings and although it is sensible to allocate a suitable sitting area on a design, the choice of seats, which is inevitably a personal affair, comes much later. Some seats, however, can be a permanent feature, like those built in with a barbecue. If you are lucky enough to have mature trees in a garden, these can make the perfect host for a large rectangular or hexagonal seat. Close to a house the former shape would be a natural choice (see Figure 8.4). The size should be ample, about 1.8 m × 1.8 m being a minimum. This will allow the surface to double as a table, play surface or even sun-lounger, provided plenty of cushions are at hand.

PERGOLAS

Pergolas are often called pagodas and vice versa. The latter are Chinese buildings and unsuitable for most gardens, except Kew, which has a beauty. Pergolas are a series of arches that cover a path or walkway and act as hosts to climbing plants. They are a traditional English feature and allow climbers to develop in the open without the restrictions of an adjoining wall that can limit both sunshine and rainfall. They can divide various parts of a garden, frame or view or act as a focal point in their own right.

Keep the construction simple. Stout timber uprights with solid beams between look better than tatty rustic

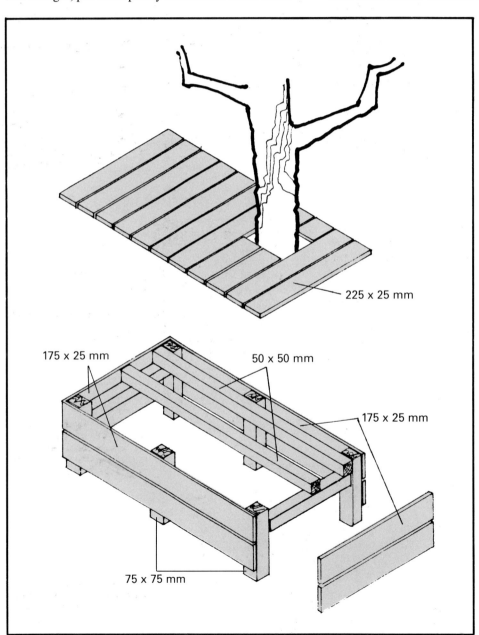

Figure 8.4 A large seat around a tree can double as a table or play surface. Timber can be stained or painted and the shape varied to fit in with the overall garden pattern.

poles or enormous brick piers.

When you consider planting, stick to a single species or theme. A single colour of rose or a collection of clematis will both look superb, while the large leaves of *Vitis coignetiae* are particularly spectacular. The neatest support for a climber is a series of wires run through vine eyes or around galvanised nails (see Figure 8.5).

OVERHEAD BEAMS

While a pergola is a free-standing structure, overhead beams normally run out from a house or high garden wall. They can be particularly useful for casting light shade over a sitting area and they can also break the line of sight from higher windows in adjoining properties. As with pergolas, use a simple construction; 22.5 cm × 5 cm floor joists are ideal and you can slot them into galvanised hangers from an adjoining wall. Scaffold poles, painted black, make an ideal support at the front, and they can be plugged with a wooden dowel and attached to the beams by means of a double-ended screw (see Figure 8.6).

The beams can be either painted or simply stained with a wood preservative, but never creosote because this would damage the plants. Such a structure makes an ideal host for climbers, supported as above.

ARBOURS

An arbour is really a hybrid between a pergola and over-head beams. It is a free-standing structure, usually positioned some way from the house, over a separate sitting area. It really makes a little secret garden and as such can be tucked away in an attractive corner. Roses are traditionally used to cover the beams but other climbers can be equally effective. With both arbours and overhead beams resist the urge to cover them with corrugated plastic. Although this may keep off the occasional shower, any rain sounds like thunder, drumming on the surface. Leaves also gather on top, quickly turn to slime and are particularly difficult to remove.

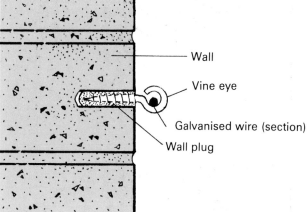

Figure 8.5 Wiring a wall for climbers. Vine eyes or masonry nails are fixed into the wall and strands of galvanised or plastic-coated wire attached.

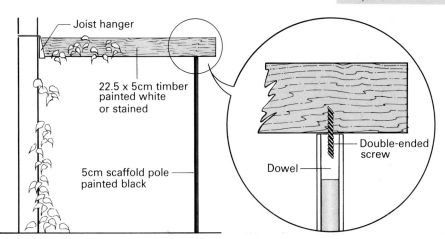

Figure 8.6 Overhead beams can be made from floor joists, supported by a scaffold pole at the front and a galvanised joist hanger from the wall.

SUMMER-HOUSES AND CONSERVATORIES

While conservatories usually adjoin a building, summer-houses are normally positioned some way away. Don't site them just anywhere; tie them into the design and make them a focal point from the house or other important viewpoint. Try to steer clear of some of the flimsy types, which are little better than a poorly constructed shed, and beware of Austrian chalets which look more at home in the Tyrol!

Conservatories are enjoying something of a revival and rightly so as they form the perfect link between inside and out, particularly when filled with foliage. Some of the contemporary designs are a little austere and limiting in size, but they can look good next to a modern house. There are now some excellent Victorian reproductions being made and these look marvellous adjoining a period house. Again, plan your hard landscape around them and do not just slap them down on an existing terrace of crazy paving, which would simply be degrading.

GAZEBOS

Gazebos were little garden buildings sited to look out over a particularly fine vista. Today the term is more often used to denote a small summer-house, usually in traditional style, that can act as a focal point within the garden. The former treatment is perfect if you have a view; and to be able to sit and contemplate it is one of the great pleasures of gardening.

PLAY AREAS

Children usually dominate a garden and a motley collection of swings, slide, sandpit and assorted wheeled toys does nothing to enhance the overall picture. Of course, the latter are going to be used all over the place, particularly on paths and other hard surfaces. It can be useful to have a large built-in cupboard or shed in which to store them. The more permanent play equipment can be specifically sited to fit into the overall pattern. A separate lawn, screened by a hedge or planting, might be ideal. An orchard is even better because the rougher grass accepts rather more wear than a lawn and the trees can act as host for a soundly built tree-house or swing. Children love mystery and seclusion and although mum likes to know where they are it can make sense to allow them their own secret area. Wendy houses are not altogether handsome little buildings, particularly those bought off the peg, and they are best hidden.

Sand pits, on the other hand, which are usually monopolised by toddlers, should always be positioned under mother's watchful eye. Outside kitchen windows is a favourite place, provided it is sunny, and if you construct the sandpit by removing several slabs within a paved area you can sweep up the sand easily in the evening. A raised sandpit is often a good idea and this could become a pool or bed later on. As nocturnal feline visitors are inevitably a problem, fit a removable cover that can be neatly slotted into position when the pit is not in use.

LIGHTING AND POWER

Electricity is something which has transformed gardens over the last 100 years. Apart from its use in the greenhouse for soil-warming, propagation, automatic irrigation and much more, it is essential for lighting, powering pumps and driving an increasingly large range of machinery.

In decorative terms lighting springs immediately to mind, although straightforward spot or flood lights are sensible in key areas both for illumination and as an all-important burglar deterrent.

On a technical front, lighting systems are usually 12 volt, the power being stepped down by a transformer inside the house (see Figure 8.7). This should be wired back to a separate fuse in the main fuse box and is a job best left to a qualified electrician. Any cables in the garden

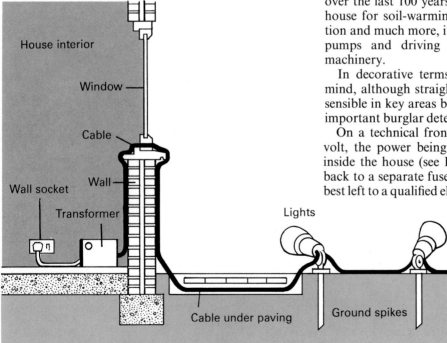

Figure 8.7 A typical low-voltage electrical system that can be used to power lighting or a submersible pool pump.

should be deeply buried and it makes sense either to run the wires through a plastic pipe or to cover them with a row of tiles, to avoid accidental damage by tools.

As in other areas of design, keep things simple. A few carefully positioned lights have far more dramatic impact than something resembling the Blackpool Illuminations. There are two basic areas involved, those close to the house and those in the more distant parts of the garden.

House lighting

House lights should echo rather than detract from an architectural style and there is nothing worse than a pair of pseudo coach lamps on a modern semi. There are an increasing number of well-designed contemporary fittings available, so use them rather than something having dubious historical connotations. Genuine or reproduction street lights on cast iron columns are equally out of place and scale in most gardens. On a terrace, background lighting of barbecue or steps is both decorative and practical. In the latter situation keep the illumination close to the ground: it is the change of level you want to see, not the top of your head.

Garden lighting

Further away from the house planting can be illuminated from both low and high levels, the latter involving lights set in trees. On the ground, lights are usually attached to spikes that can be moved about and the siting of these is really a two-person job, with one in the house looking at the effect and one doing the manipulation. Remember that you have an opportunity to give the garden a quite different character and many ground lights show the underside of leaves which are not normally visible during daytime. The colour of the lights is important: stick to white or blue; some of the reds, yellow and oranges turn foliage a sickly hue.

Pool lighting

As far as pool lighting is concerned the same basic rule of simplicity applies. One or two lights anchored on the bottom gives an attractive, diffused glow, but the floating, rotating, holographic displays are disturbing to say the least.

FURNISHINGS

Pots and containers (see Figure 8.8)

These really are garden furnishings and should be treated as such. While you may see a corner or position when working out a plan, the final siting becomes obvious once the garden is built. The choice is legion and personal. It can range from contemporary shapes in brightly coloured plastic, through cement and terracotta, to timber half-barrels and window boxes. All will have their place and by now you should have a feeling for what looks right in a particular setting!

Groups of pots usually look better than single containers dotted about at random. In many situations the type of pot becomes incidental, foliage flopping over the

Figure 8.8 A selection of pots that would be suitable in a wide range of garden settings.

edges to mask virtually everything below. This means that nearly anything can be effective: old buckets, bins and even a bath tub could be used, the latter providing leg room for a really worthwhile display.

This question of size is important. The bigger the pot the better, as there is more available space for root development and watering need not be carried out as often as for a small container, which will dry out quickly. Bear in mind also that here is an opportunity to provide specialised growing conditions and you could prepare a peaty, acid soil suitable for ericaceous plants that might not grow elsewhere in the garden.

Statues and ornaments

Like pots, the range of statues and ornaments is enormous, from classical pieces that have a genuinely high price, right through to garden gnomes. While the purist shudders at the latter, there is nothing wrong with a sense of humour in the garden and a brightly coloured fellow leaning on a rake or fishing endlessly in a pool is quite simply funny. Added to that, children love it!

Coming back to reality, the siting of a statue is a tricky business and something that can be done on the drawing board. Such a piece will fit sensibly in a niche or the angle formed by two walls, foliage framing a bust or figure to further enhance the picture. Like conifers, statues are punctuation marks and a surfeit becomes restless, so choose and use them carefully.

Ornamentation need not necessarily be man-made. A large, smooth rock carefully positioned on the corner of a bed, or projecting into a paved area is pure sculpture. A fallen tree, shaped up and placed by a woodland walk doubles as both a dramatic statement and a seat, while a bold-leaved climber can transform a great ball of tangled chicken wire into a huge green boulder. This ability to look at things in a different light and act accordingly is one of the arts of garden design.

CHECKPOINT

Having read this chapter you should have successfully sited your chosen features, taking into account their relationship with other parts of the garden, and should be able to use your knowledge of materials and rules of design to carry out any construction work.

To check that you have understood the points made in this chapter, answer the following questions.

1 What size, shape and depth would you recommend for an ornamental pool sited close to a paved terraced area?
2 If you wanted to construct your own ornamental pool, what material could you use which would be both easy to handle and likely to last for many years?
3 How can you calculate the amount of liner you will need to construct your pool?
4 How often should you drain and clean out an ornamental pool?
5 What kind of water feature is the safest to install in a garden used by very young children?
6 Which design rules apply when you are choosing the shape of a swimming pool?
7 What situation would you be endeavouring to echo if you built a rockery in your garden?
8 What type of planting is recommended for a pergola?
9 At what height should you site lighting on steps?
10 At what stage in the planning and construction of your garden should you include pots and containers and why?

Check your answers against the information in this chapter.

CHAPTER NINE

Maintenance and modification

Caring for tools/Caring for planting/Caring for hard surfaces
Modifying your garden/Checkpoint

It is all very well designing and building a handsome garden, but once it is complete somebody is going to have to look after it, and that's probably going to be *you*.

Again, some of the sections in this chapter may not be applicable to your garden so they are listed in Table 9.1, together with the numbers of the pages on which they can be found, so that you can turn easily to the sections you need.

Table 9.1 **Maintenance and modification of your garden**

If you have gone about your design sensibly, tailoring it to fit your own personal requirements, maintenance will hopefully be set at an acceptable level. In general terms maintenance is common sense, but to make sense you really need to know how materials work and how they are laid. It is also fair to say that maintenance on a regular basis is a comfortable job, while, if it is left too long, it simply becomes a chore. In many ways this is the key to gardening: little and often is not only far more effective than a back-breaking blitz once in a blue moon, but also immeasurably more enjoyable.

CARING FOR TOOLS

The maintenance work that you do have to carry out can be made less arduous and time-consuming if the tools you use are always kept in peak condition.

Handtools

Spades and other handtools should always be kept clean and sharp. Stainless steel, although expensive, provides a marvellous cutting edge. Digging becomes a joy and you will find that you can work land that is difficult to move with conventional tools.

Mowers

As far as mowers in general are concerned the rules are simple. Keep them lightly oiled and remove wet grass after use to minimise rust.

Always keep the plug of a motor mower clean. With a two-stroke machine, pay particular attention to this as oiling-up is a common problem.

Inspect the blades of cylinder mowers regularly and if any of these become bent, carefully straighten them with a hammer. File out burrs on the blades and arrange for regular sharpening by a local dealer to make sure that the cut remains clean.

Winter storage in the wrong conditions often leads to problems the following spring and a few simple rules save endless frustration.

a Disconnect the fuel line from the carburettor and let the machine run dry. This ensures that the former stays clean and dry throughout the winter.

b Turn the engine over so that it comes on to the compression stroke. This closes the valves, keeping the cylinder dry, and also closes the points so that these remain clean.

c Store in damp-free conditions, if possible. This applies to the storage of all equipment.

CARING FOR PLANTING

Hoeing and weeding

Much of the work in the average garden involves hoeing and weeding borders, though a good planting plan will do much to reduce this labour. Bear in mind, however, that there will be quite a lot to do initially in keeping the ground clear between developing plants. This is time well spent as it minimises competition by weeds and allows plants to knit together quickly. Such work will thus be on a sliding scale and can be reduced by sensible mulching with organic manure or chipped bark.

Grass-cutting

Grass-cutting is perhaps the job that involves most time. By eliminating awkward shapes and allowing easy access to all parts of the lawn savings can be made here too.

Pruning

Apart from the tending of plants at ground level, a certain amount of pruning will need to be undertaken. There is enormous mystery about this but really the job is relatively simple: it involves keeping a shrub or tree to manageable proportions with an attractive overall appearance. This takes us back to planting design and underlines the point that you must be aware of the eventual size of any subject. The horrendous hacking of forest trees in a small garden is an all too familiar sight and simply results from the wrong species being used in the first place.

Trees

Tree surgery (Figure 9.1) is a sensitive business and should be confined to the removal of dead and diseased wood or the judicious shaping of an untidy specimen. Branches should always be removed cleanly and this should be carried out in two stages. First, cut the branch back to relieve as much weight as possible, and then trim the stump back to the trunk. Until recently the application of a sealant was considered prudent but recent trials have shown this to be unnecessary. Never leave a jagged or torn cut, though, as this simply invites disease and accelerates decay. As a general rule, thin out the canopy by removing some branches completely. Never hack them all back as if you were giving the tree a haircut.

With the toll taken by Dutch elm disease there are still a lot of extremely dangerous trees left standing. The removal of these is not a job for amateurs and should be left to qualified tree surgeons. In this case beware of the cowboy operator, often without insurance, who can create very expensive havoc. Trees look relatively safe when standing, but can be terrifying falling in the wrong direction.

Shrubs

As far as shrubs are concerned, the time of pruning really depends on the flowering season. Hydrangeas or buddleias flower late in the year and should therefore be cut back in the spring so that there is ample time for young wood to develop. Buddleias in particular can be cut back hard as they have a tendency to get more and more leggy if pruned only lightly.

Subjects that flower earlier in the year, during the spring and early summer, should be pruned after

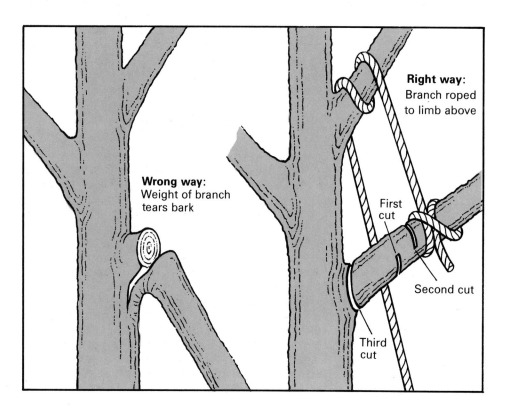

Wrong way:
Weight of branch tears bark

Right way:
Branch roped to limb above

First cut

Second cut

Third cut

Figure 9.1 Tree surgery. The illustration on the left shows an incorrect cut, where the weight of the branch has ripped the bark down the trunk. On the right as much weight as possible has been removed and the remaining part of the branch roped to a secure limb above to take its weight while the final cut is made.

flowering; cytisus (broom) is a good example of this.

Taller deciduous shrubs, typified by lilac or viburnums, can simply be thinned out every three or four years, removing any old, weak or diseased shoots entirely.

Ground cover should remain just that and many varieties get straggly unless clipped over in April; this includes heathers and heaths that need to remain tight in order to knit together.

A final group are the shrubs, such as dogwood and willow, that are grown for the winter colour of their stems. As this colour is shown to best effect on the new wood, they should be cut back to within a couple of buds of the old wood in March.

Roses

Roses are in a class of their own and hybrid tea and floribunda bush roses are pruned hard back to just below knee height. Prune to an outward facing bud and never be afraid of doing a thorough job. Look in your local park to see how it is done. March is the latest time to carry this out, although long stems that might break in the winter gales can be cut back by half in November. Climbing and rambling roses only need lightly pruning if they outgrow their allotted space. Dead wood, dead flowerheads and one or two older stems can be removed, but otherwise leave them alone.

Herbaceous plants

Herbaceous plants that will probably form part of the overall planting scheme should also be divided every three or four years, as the best blooms are often produced from the newer shoots. As a general rule, lift, divide and replant the early flowering varieties in autumn and the later flowering subjects in spring. The healthiest parts of a hardy perennial are around the outside of a clump and these should be used. The dead central section is best thrown away. A few types (heuchera, for instance) have a habit of growing progressively further out of the ground. This results in a loss of flower. They can be divided in a similar way to the above and replanted at a deeper level.

Moving plants

Inevitably there are gaps in borders that need filling, or plants may need moving for other reasons. Deciduous shrubs can be safely planted or transplanted throughout their dormant season, roughly from November to March, as long as the ground is not completely waterlogged or solid with frost. Coniferous plants and evergreens in general should be moved during the latter part of March or in April.

In basic terms, the larger the specimen, the harder it is to move, and the greater the preparation needed. Cut around mature shrubs with a spade several weeks before they are to be moved. This reduces the shock to their system at planting time. In many cases a young plant will re-establish far more quickly than a mature specimen, quickly overhauling the latter with greater vigour. Any freshly moved plant needs adequate aftercare: water it if the earth is dry and stake it if there is any chance of wind damage.

Lawns

I considered the laying and general care of lawns in Chapter 6, 'Soft landscape', but one or two further points may be helpful. Bare patches in an inherited garden are common and, to many, puzzling. The problem could be a chunk of buried hardcore – not uncommon in new properties – or it could be a buried manhole cover or even a concrete path! Whatever the cause, investigation will be necessary. This will involve lifting the dead turf and any underlying soil. If hardcore is involved simply remove this and backfill with clean topsoil, firming this down well. Bring the soil up slightly higher than the previous level, to allow for natural settlement. Finally, reseed or returf.

Dogs, or more accurately bitches, have exceptionally strong urine which can leave brown patches all over the place. The obvious answer is to train the animals to go elsewhere, but if this is impossible the best solution is a hose or bucket of water – used on the fresh puddle, not the dog!

The amount of weedkilling that you should do really depends on what you find acceptable. As I have already said, a sprinkling of daisies or speedwell could enhance the overall picture. Perennial weeds may need sterner treatment, though, and various chemical spot-weeders or pointed trowels are available either to destroy them or to get them out. An easier course of action is a combined fertiliser and weedkiller that you can apply to the whole lawn in the spring or autumn.

CARING FOR HARD SURFACES

Protecting timber

Timber is widely used in the garden and our temperate, wet climate soon makes inroads if wood is left unprotected. Creosote should never be used; a suitable non-toxic preservative should be employed instead. Sheds, summerhouses, fences, pergolas and overhead beams will all need regular attention and, if well looked after, will need minimal repair. If plants are grown against any timber structure they will, of course, need taking down before preservative is applied.

Fences rot in time and posts or panels will need replacing. A long gravel board run underneath the panels can save expense as this can be renewed far more cheaply. Concrete posts are also virtually indestructible and come with slots cast in the sides to accept panels. Plain concrete looks harsh but if it is painted brown, an excellent landscape colour, it will blend well into the background

Repointing walls (see Figure 9.2)

Old walls have great charm, but were inevitably built with soft, lime mortar that crumbles away over the years. This can weaken the wall to a dangerous extent and repointing will be necessary. Place a long board at the bottom of the wall to catch bits and then rake out the old mortar to a depth of about 13 mm and brush the wall down to remove debris. Use a mix of one part cement, six parts soft sand and one part plasticiser for the new mortar. Damp the wall over an area of about 1 m² and point the vertical joints first. The style of pointing, which was covered in Chapter 4, dictates the finished look of the wall.

Replacing paving

It may be necessary from time to time to replace a paving slab or brick that has become damaged. Bricks are, of course, susceptible to frost unless well-fired. If you need to replace a brick carefully chop the old material out with a hammer and wide-headed bolster chisel, removing the mortar beneath, being careful not to disturb the surrounding surface. Mix up a small amount of mortar and bed a new brick in position, tamping this down to match the existing levels round about. The same procedure applies to replacing a larger slab.

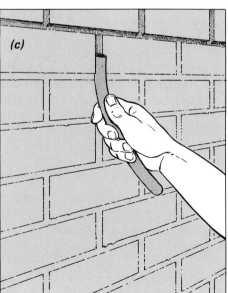

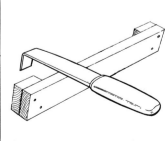
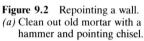

Figure 9.2 Repointing a wall.
- *(a)* Clean out old mortar with a hammer and pointing chisel.
- *(b)* Make sure the wall is damp and fill in the vertical joints first. Work in areas of about 1 m² at a time.
- *(c)* Keyed or rubbed back joints can be made with a piece of rubber pipe or a bucket handle.
- *(d)* Weathered joints should be made with a trowel and any excess mortar cleaned off with a 'Frenchman' knife (one with the end bent at a right angle) used against a straight edge.

MODIFYING YOUR GARDEN

The level of maintenance really depends on the time available and this is one thing that can change quite considerably over the years. A young family, although energetic, often has little time for regular work in the garden. Once the children have left home, or even once they go to school, the pattern changes and you may feel able to spend a lot more time outside. This is probably a point at which you want to make some changes in the way you use your garden.

Certain features that were specifically for youngsters – paddling pools or sandpits – could now become raised beds, ornamental pools or herb gardens. The sometimes considerable area given over to swings, slides and play equipment might give way first to a badminton lawn for older children and later to a vegetable garden or orchard. If the garden has been designed properly all these changes will take place naturally, without major upheavals to the structural plan. Then eventually you will have to think of retirement and a gentle slowing down. Vegetables may be too much work, in which case the lawn, or part of it, may be given over to an extension of the terrace or sitting area. But don't forget grandchildren: the swings may well reappear!

The good sense of building raised beds in the early days will be a boon now: they will not have to be built from scratch and they will be in place with the bonus of mature planting that will inevitably have taken time to develop. It is also true to say that prices for everything go up and jobs carried out in the slightly more affluent middle years can save a great deal later on.

CHECKPOINT

Now that you have read this chapter you should be able to care for your tools, plants and hard surfaces and, as time goes on, make any necessary modifications to your original design.

To check that you have understood the points made in this chapter, answer the following questions.

1 What should you do to a motor mower before storing it away for the winter?
2 At what time of year should you prune the following plants:
   a buddleia;
   b cytisus;
   c heathers;
   d willow?
3 What is the latest date for pruning roses?
4 At what time of the year can you safely move deciduous shrubs?
5 What mix would you use, and in what proportions, for mortar to repoint a wall?

Check your answers against the information in the chapter.

Further reading

Beazley, Elizabeth. *Design and Detail of the Space between Buildings* (Architectural Press: London, 1960).

Bloom, Alan. *Perennials for Trouble-free Gardening* (Faber & Faber: London, 1968).

Brookes, John, *Room Outside* (Thames & Hudson: London, 1969).

Fox, Robin Lane. *Variations on a Garden* (Macmillan: London, 1974).

Hay, Roy, and Synge, Patrick M. *The Dictionary of Garden Plants in Colour* (Michael Joseph: London, 1969).

Hilliers Manual of Trees and Shrubs (David & Charles: Newton Abbot, 1974).

Huxley, Anthony. *An Illustrated History of Gardening* (Papermac: London, 1978).

Huxley, Anthony (ed.). *Financial Times Book of Gardening* (David & Charles: Newton Abbot, 1975).

Jellicoe, Susan, and Allen, Marjory. *Town Gardens to Live in* (Penguin Books: Harmondsworth, 1977).

Millar, S. Gault. *The Dictionary of Shrubs in Colour* (Michael Joseph: London, 1976).

The Easy Path to Gardening (Readers Digest Association/Disabled Living Foundation: London, 1972).

Thomas, Graham Stuart. *Plants for Ground Cover* (Dent: London, 1970).

Index